# "Book of Rose Outlines"

All Artwork by

## *Cort Bengtson*

Published by
Cort's Royal Ink Tattoo Company
Book Design and Layout by
Cort Bengtson

Copyright  2017
All images are on file with
The Library of Congress



ISBN: 978-1-948187-12-1

# Some tips

You will notice the first 30 pages were drawn
in light gray. This is for the purpose of doing
realistic style renderings. If you look at
photographs of real roses, there is no hard
black outline. If you want to practice
your outlining for tattooing,
trace the deisgn using a slightly thicker line.


The next set of pages is done in a nice thick
black outline for doing bold tradtional tattoo
style coloring.
Challenge yourself to use colors you
normally wouldn't. Maybe even replace smooth
shading with a pattern.
I would like to challenge you to
color one in as fast as you can and then
spend as much time as you can on one.
Maybe even a couple of hours!

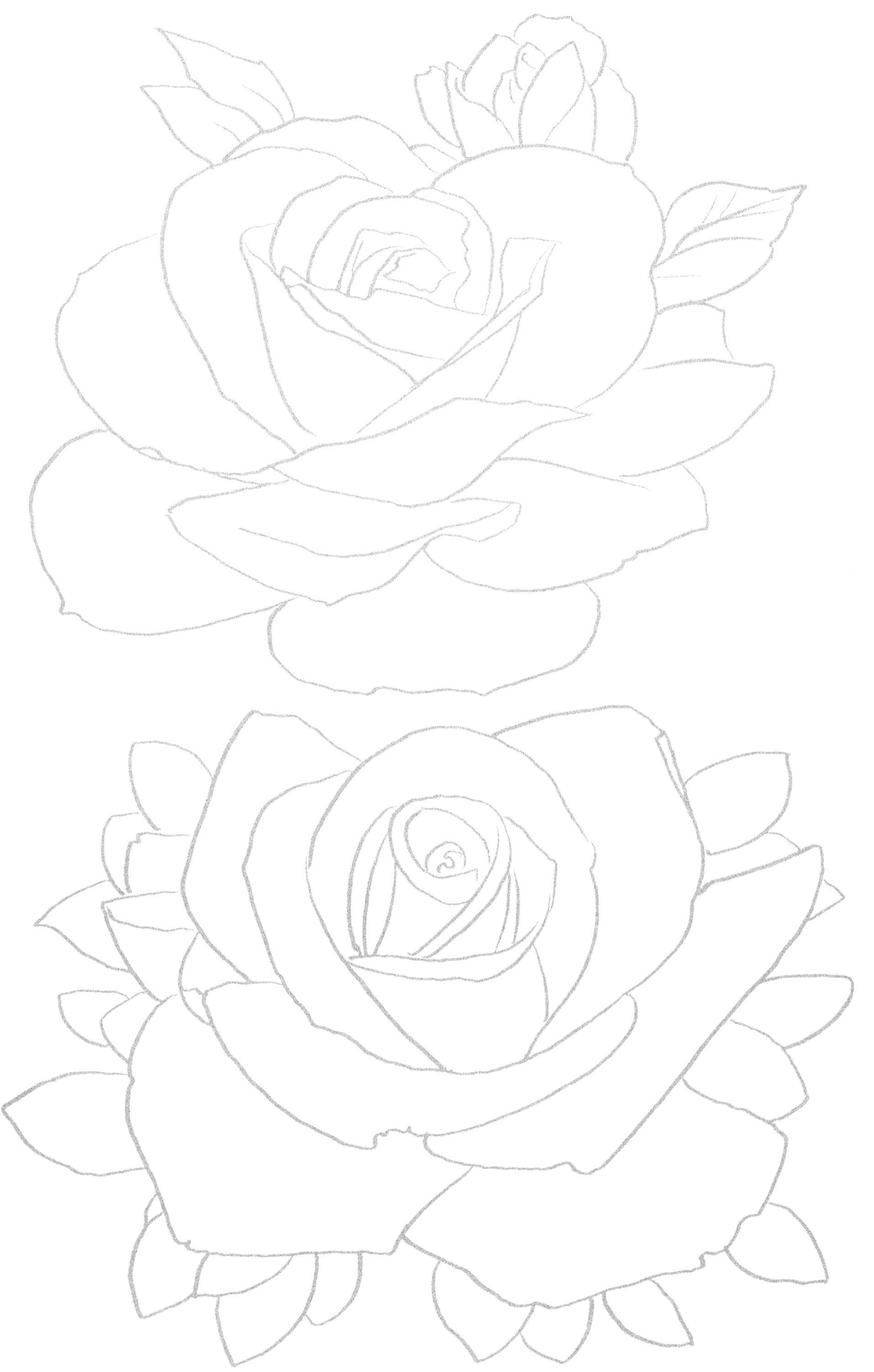

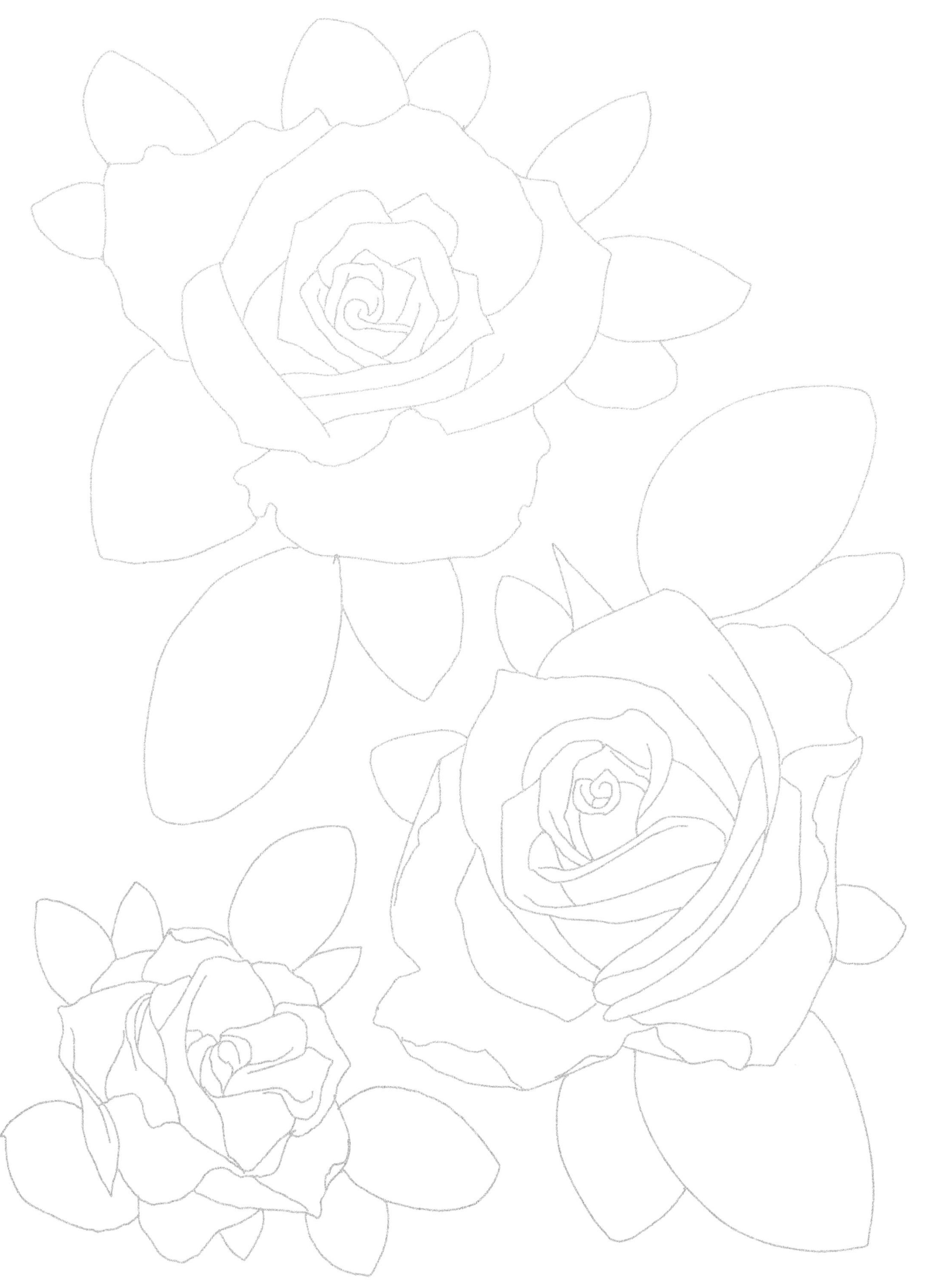

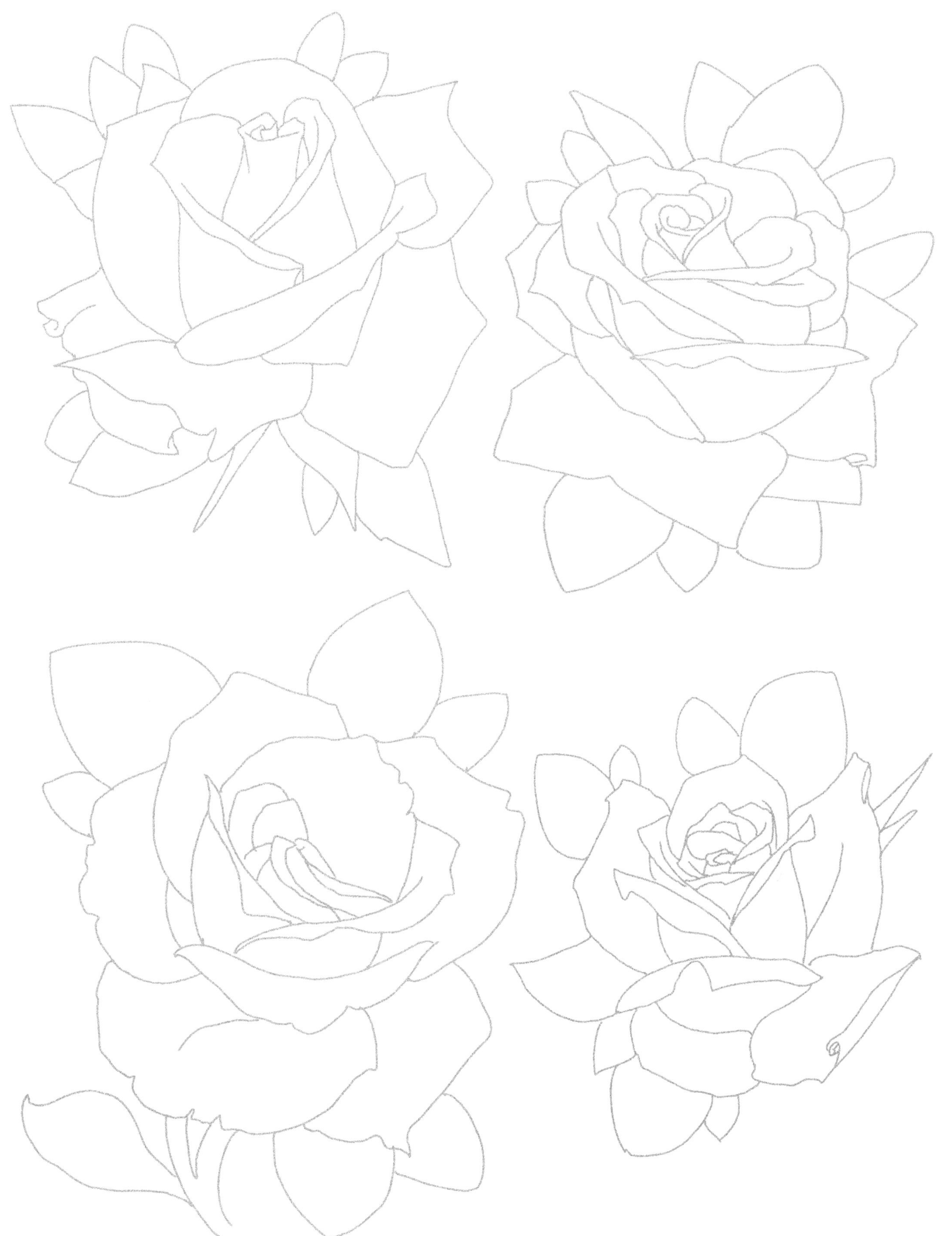

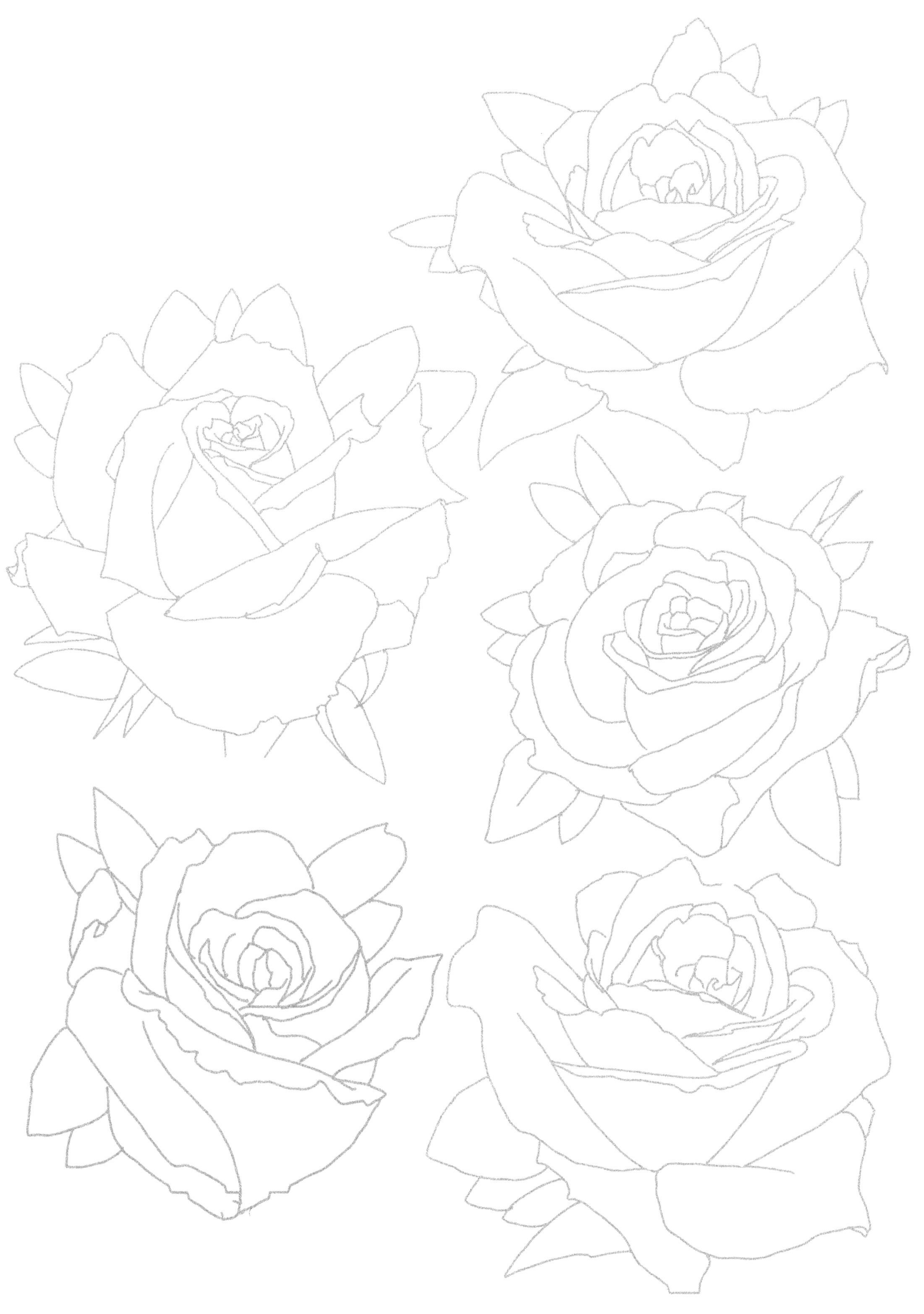

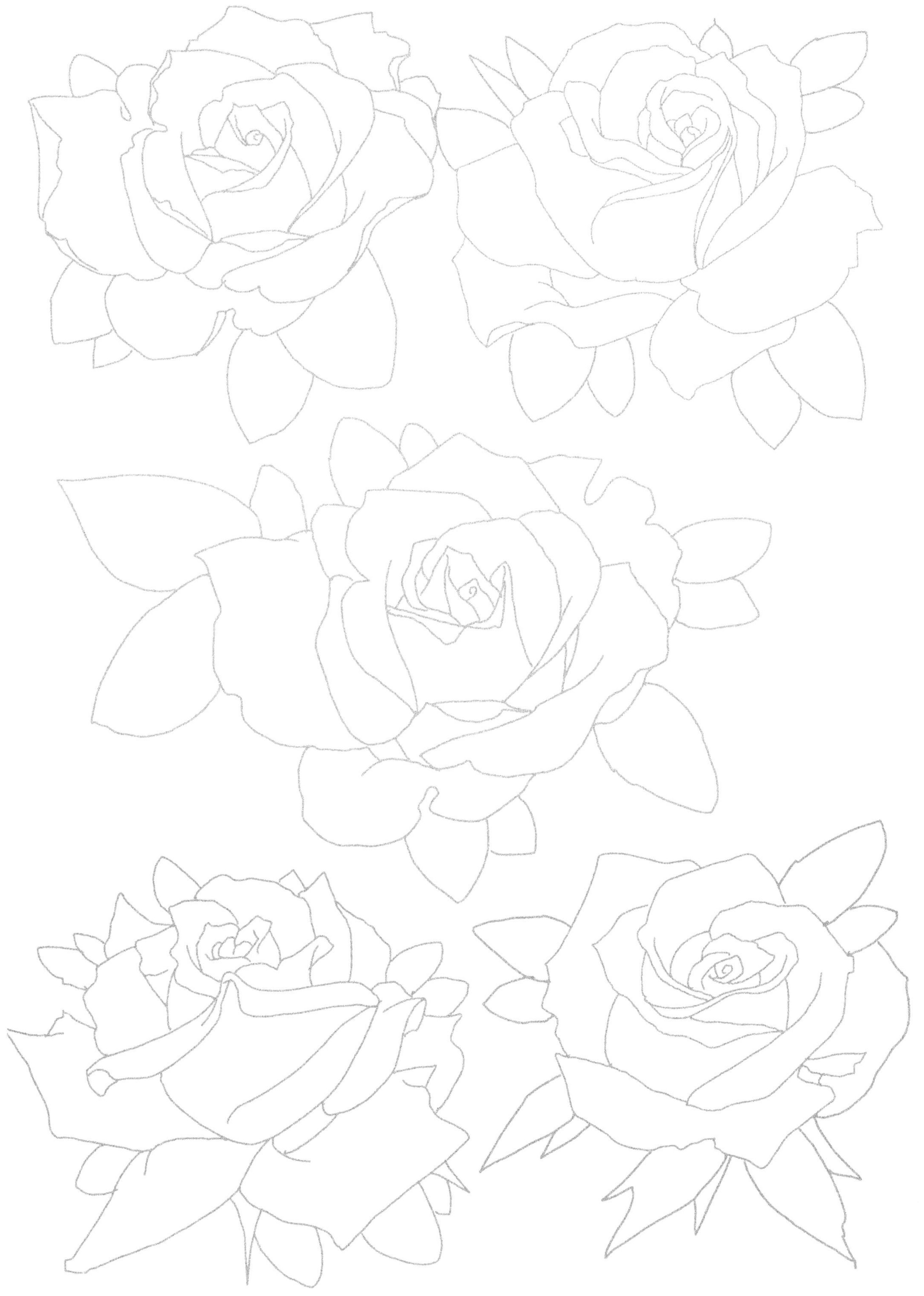

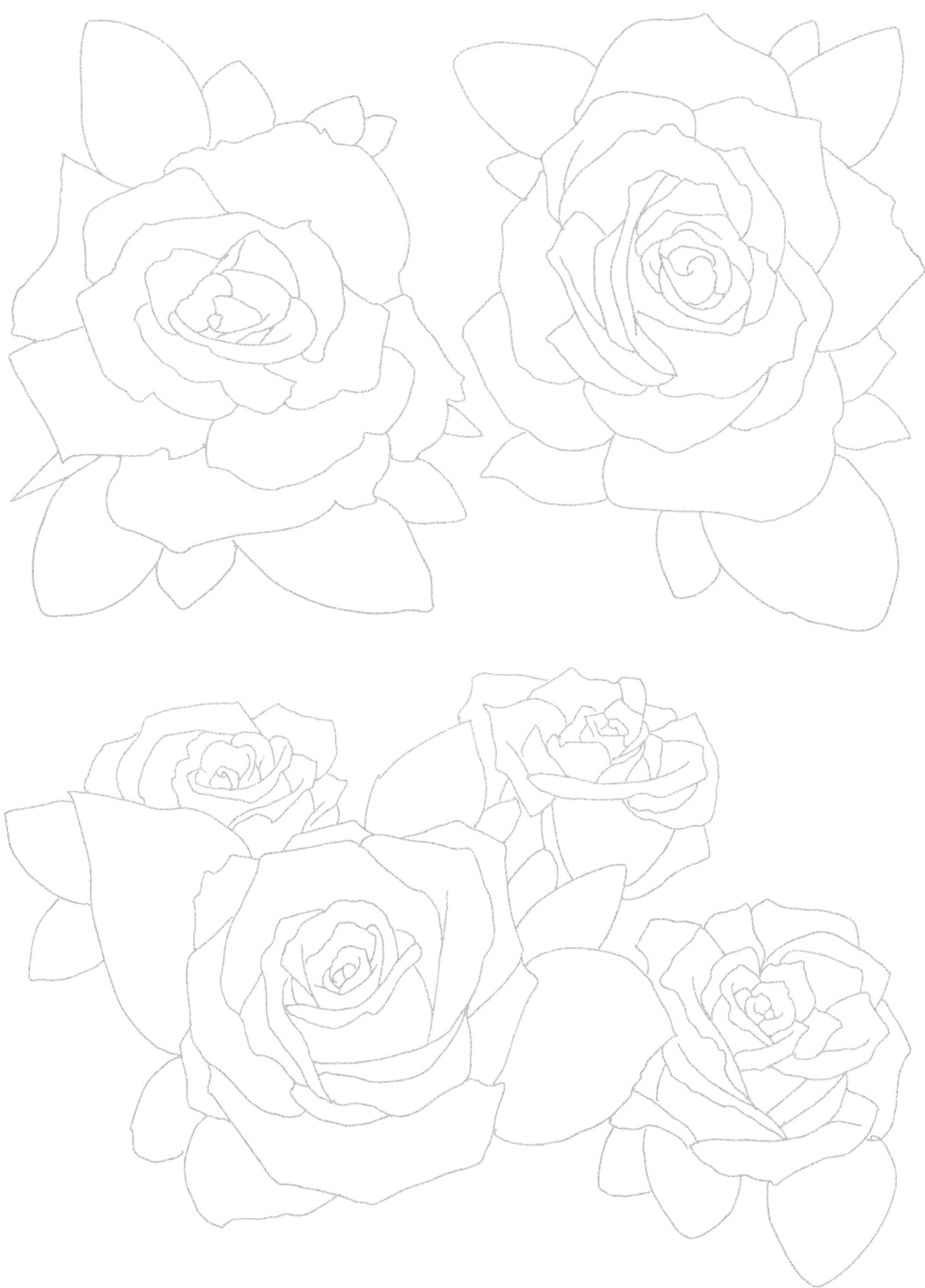

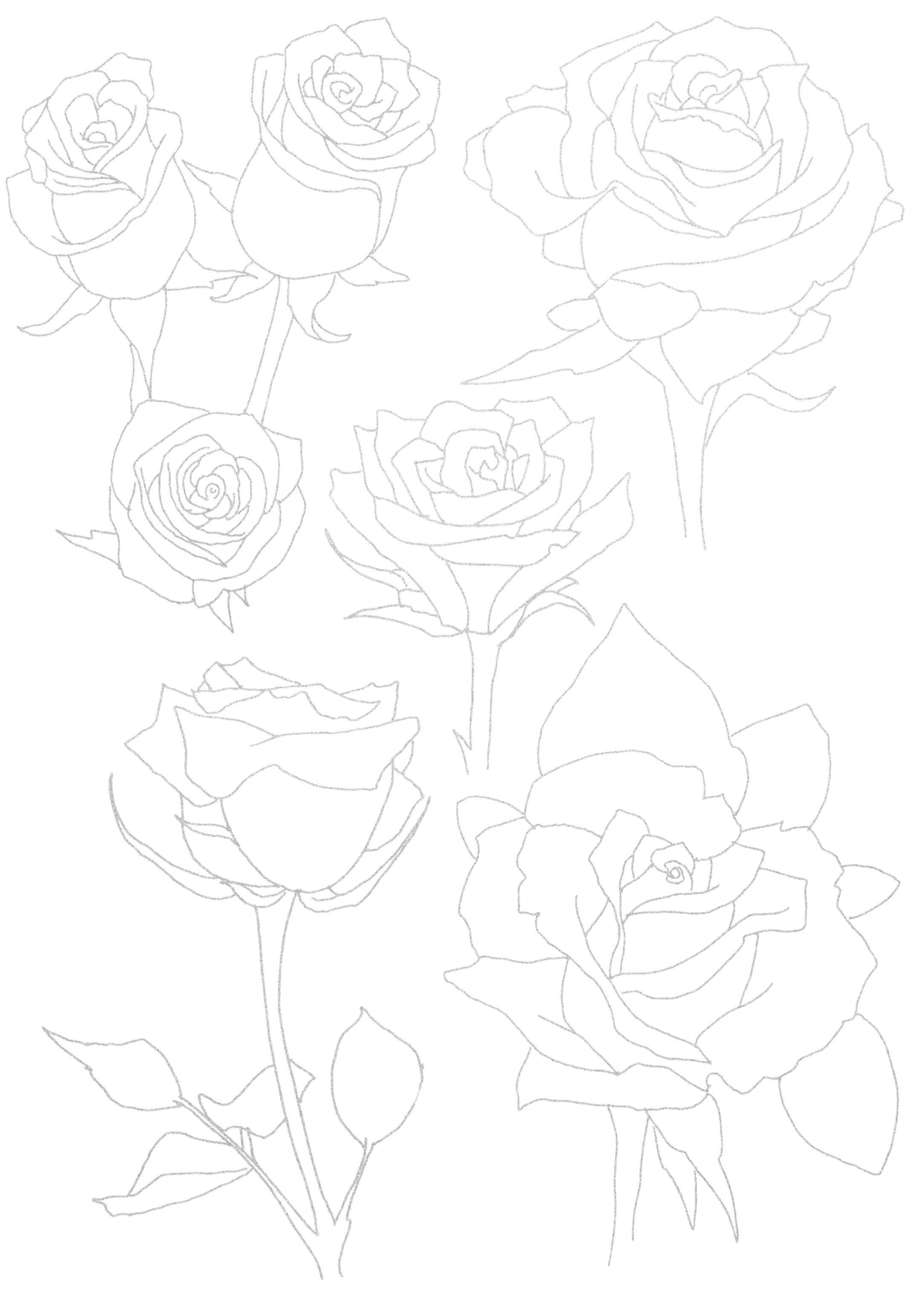

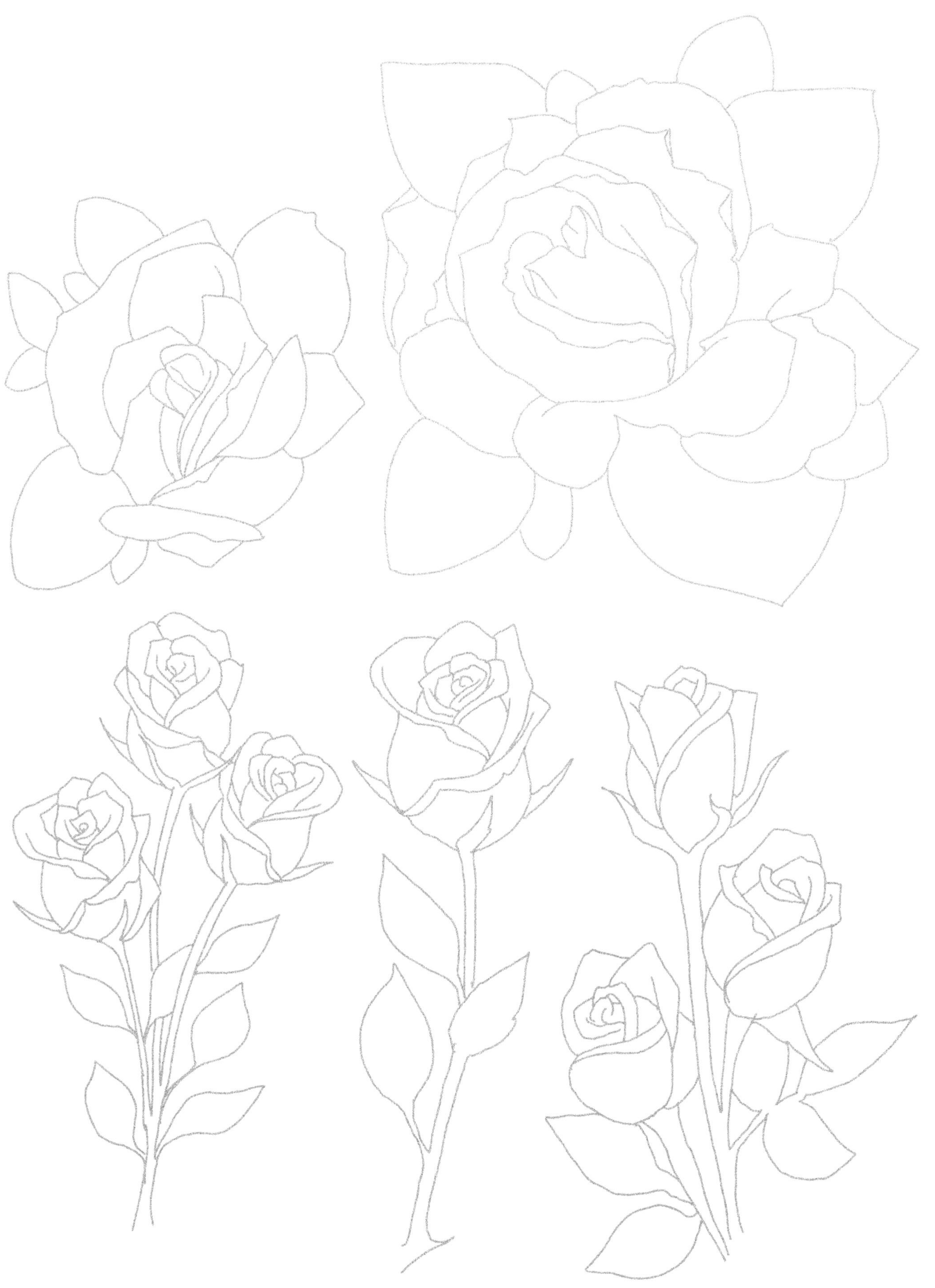

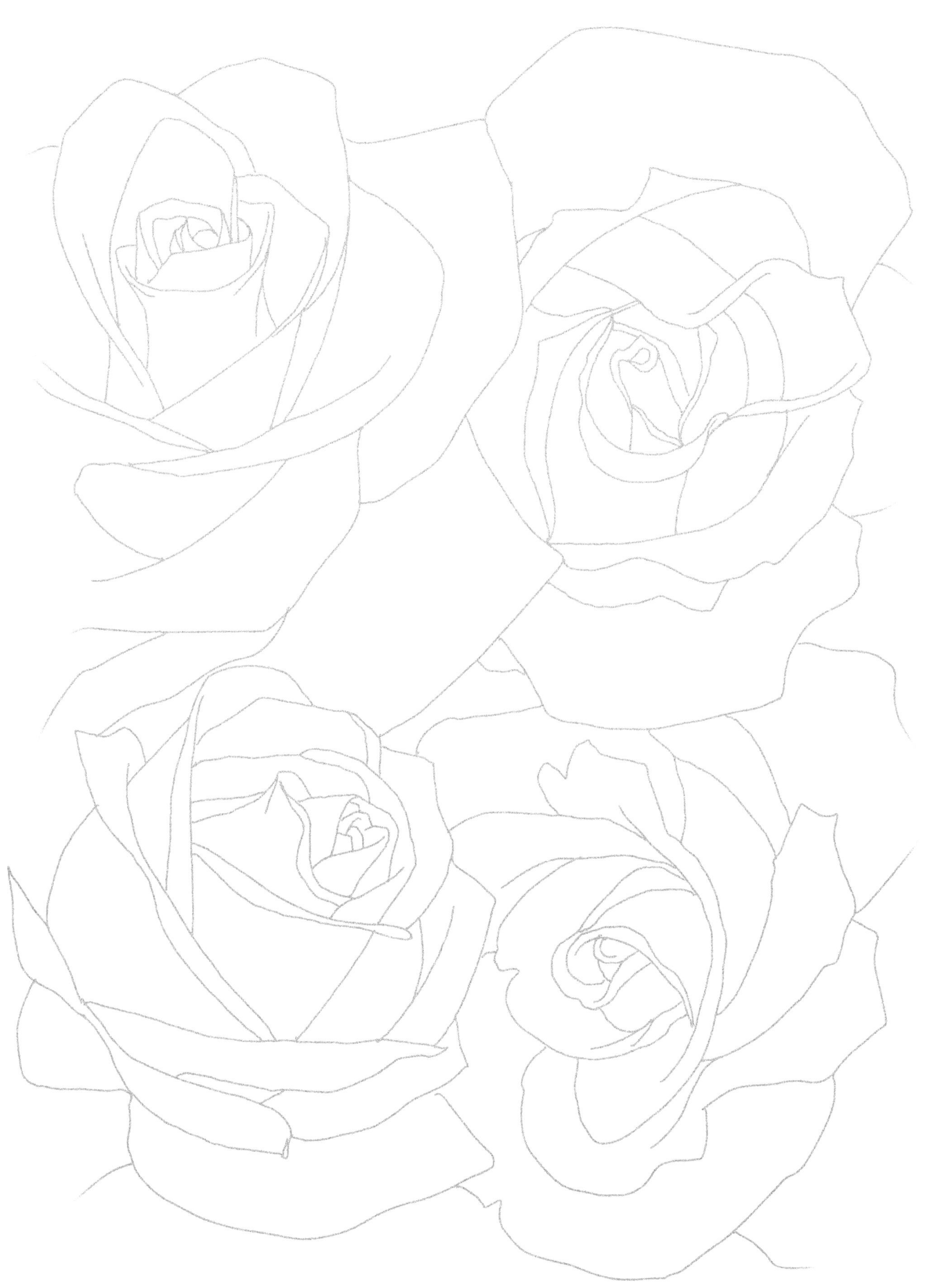

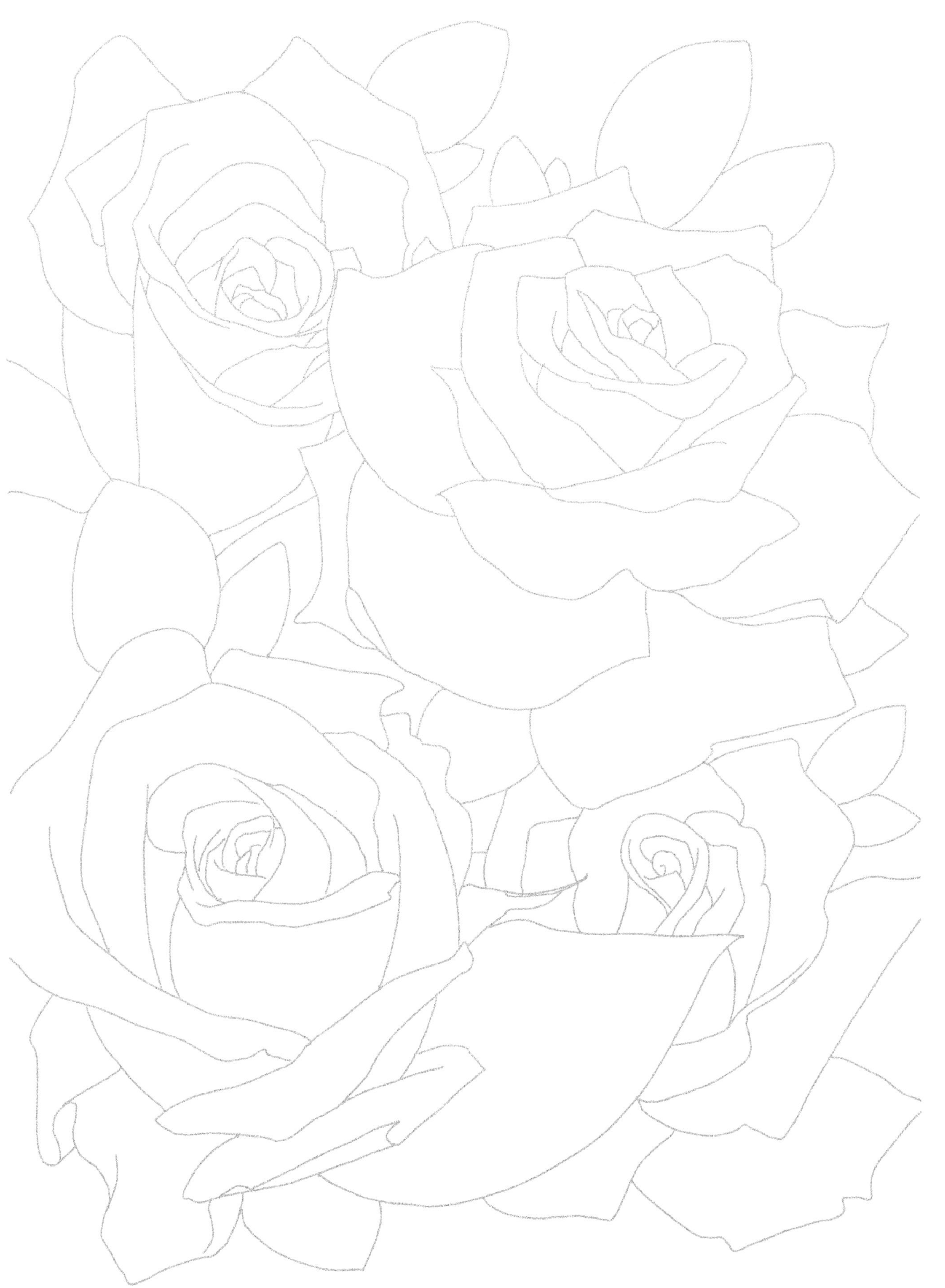

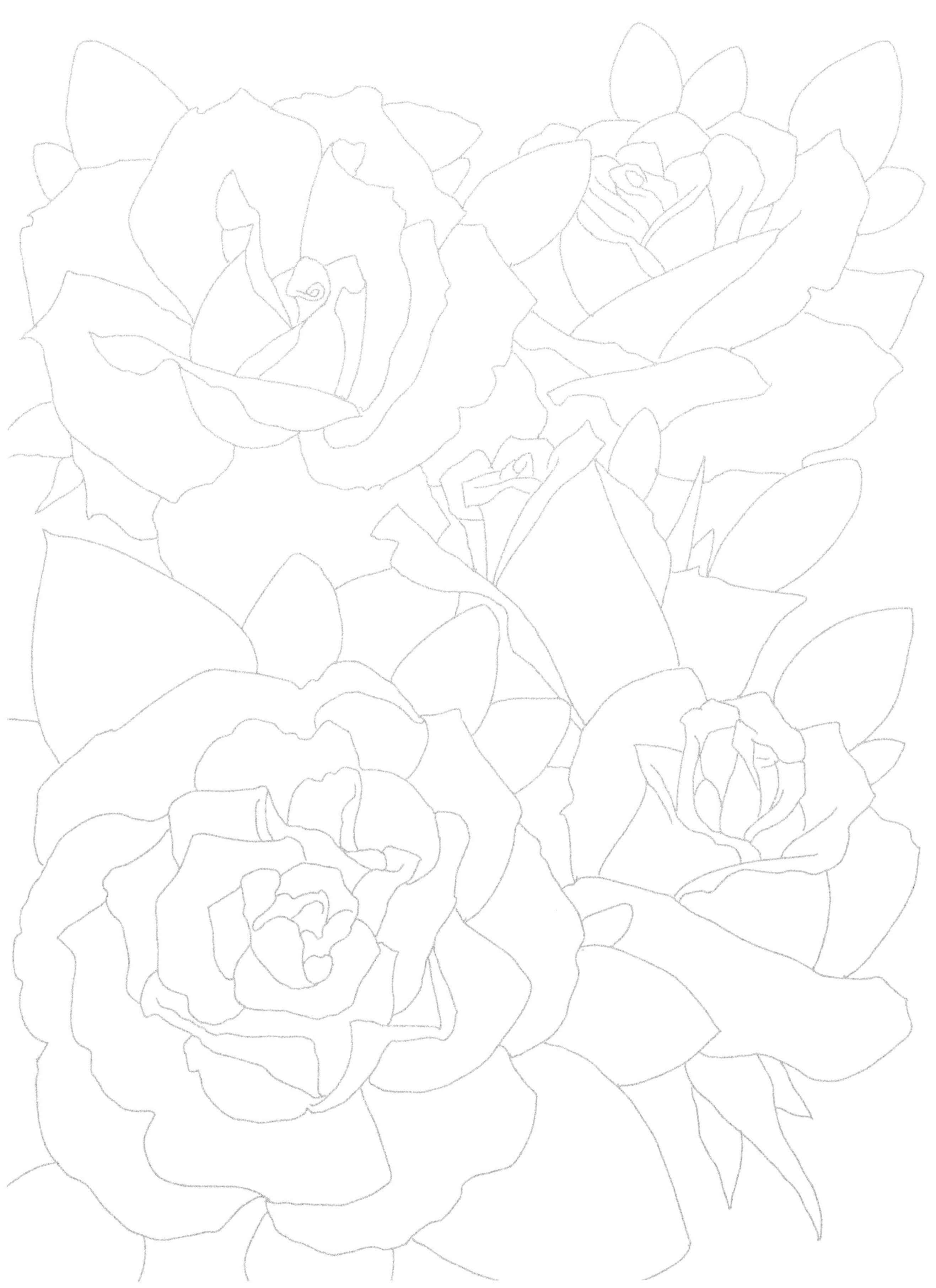

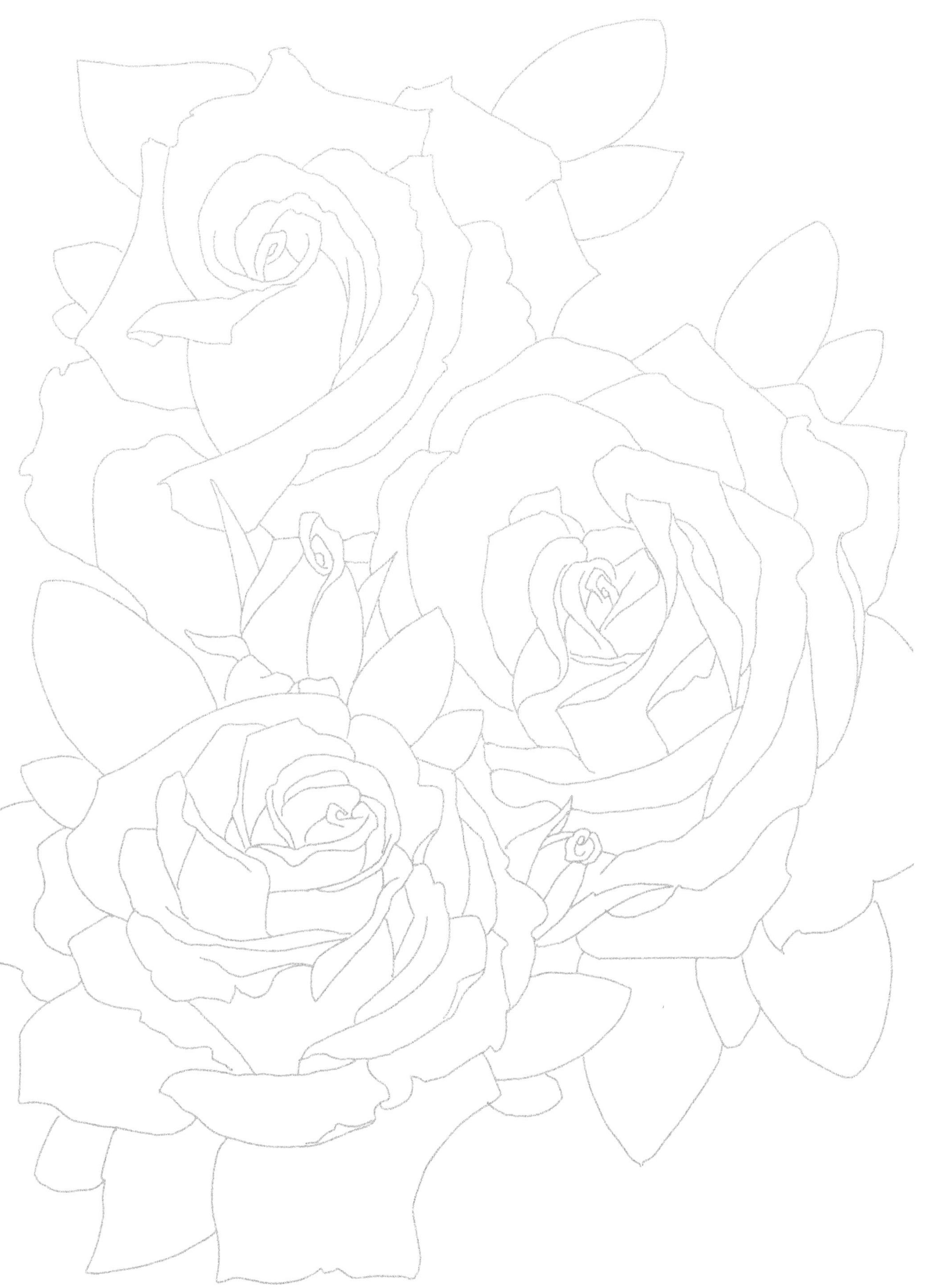

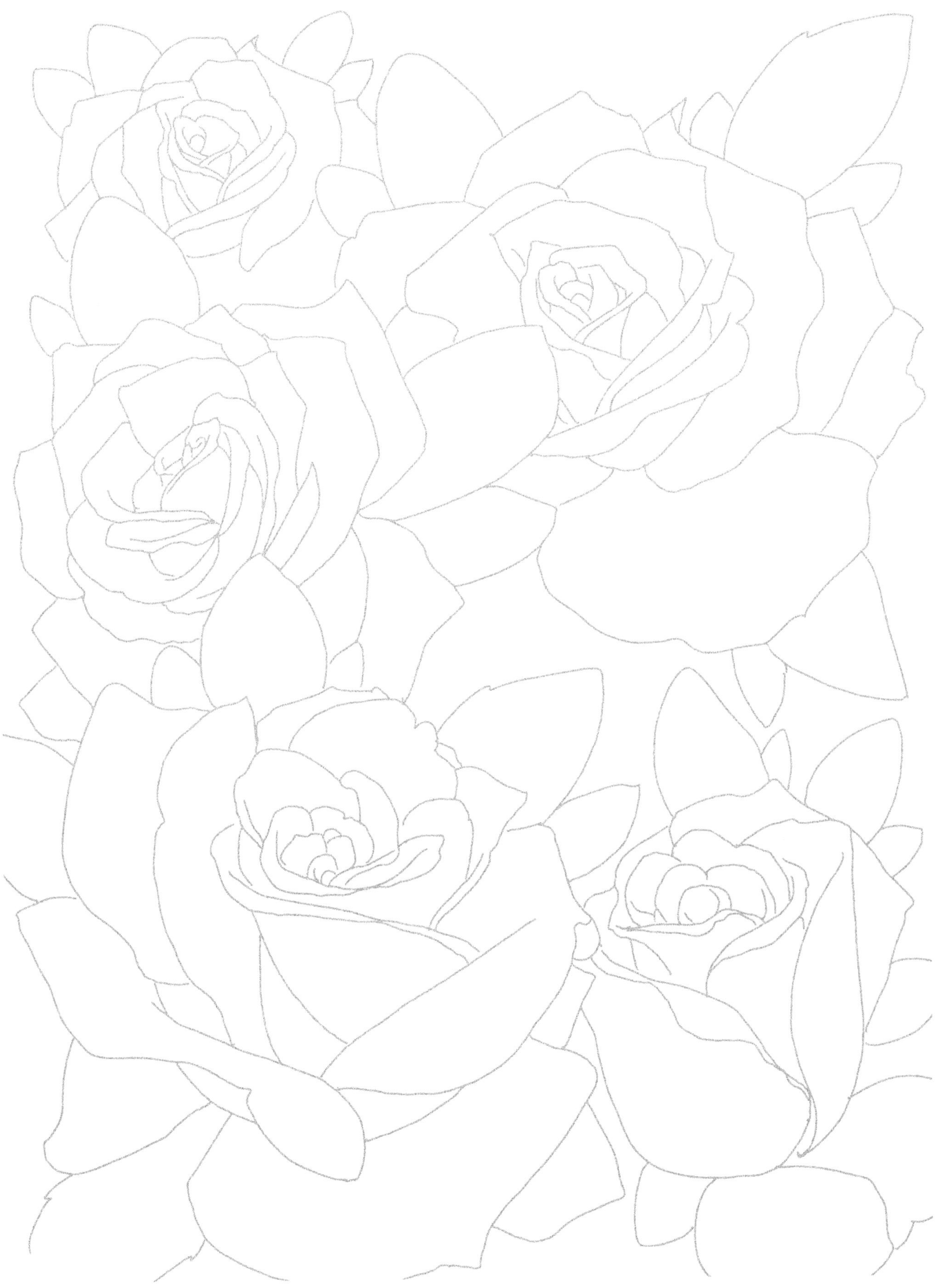

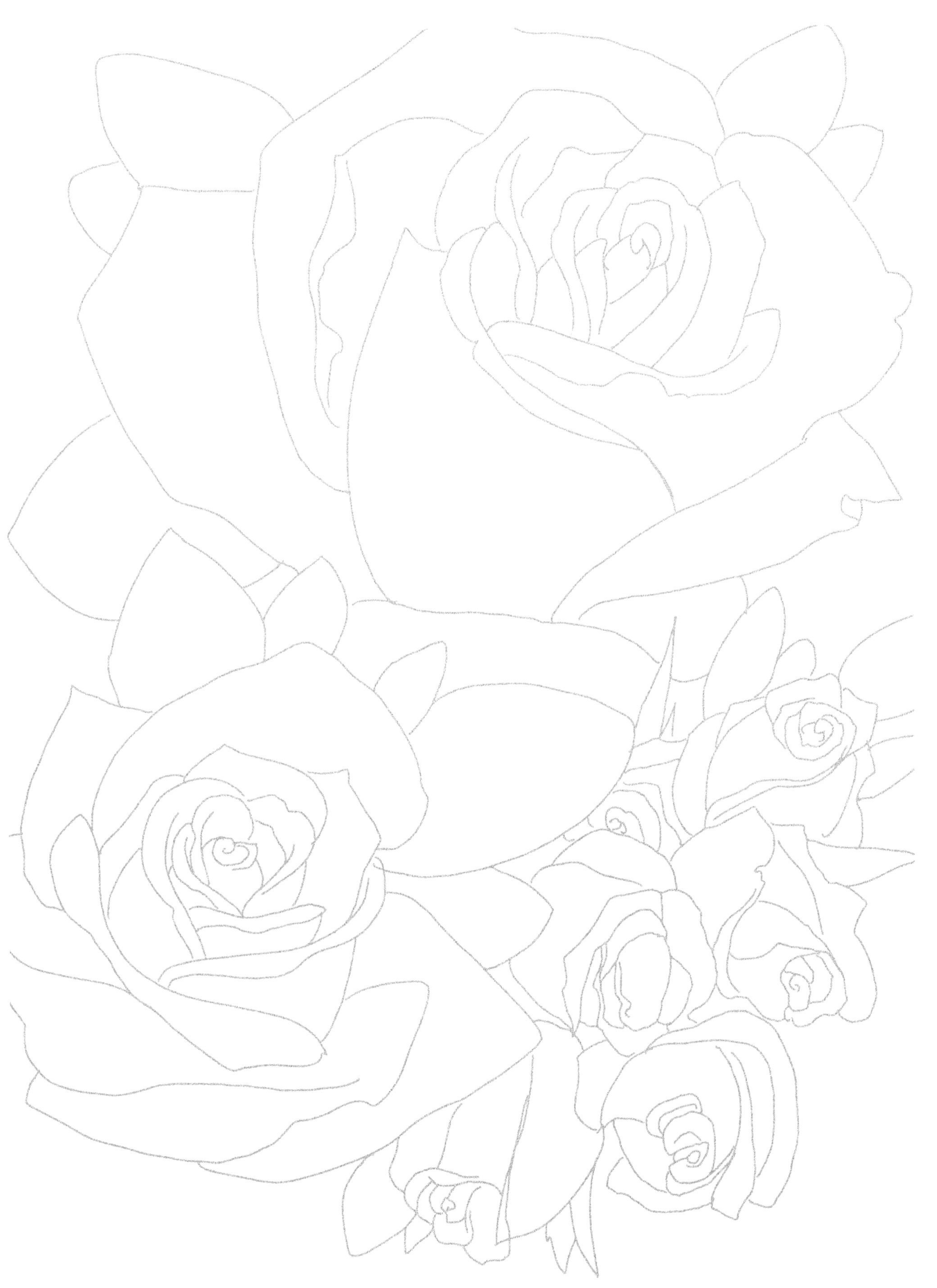

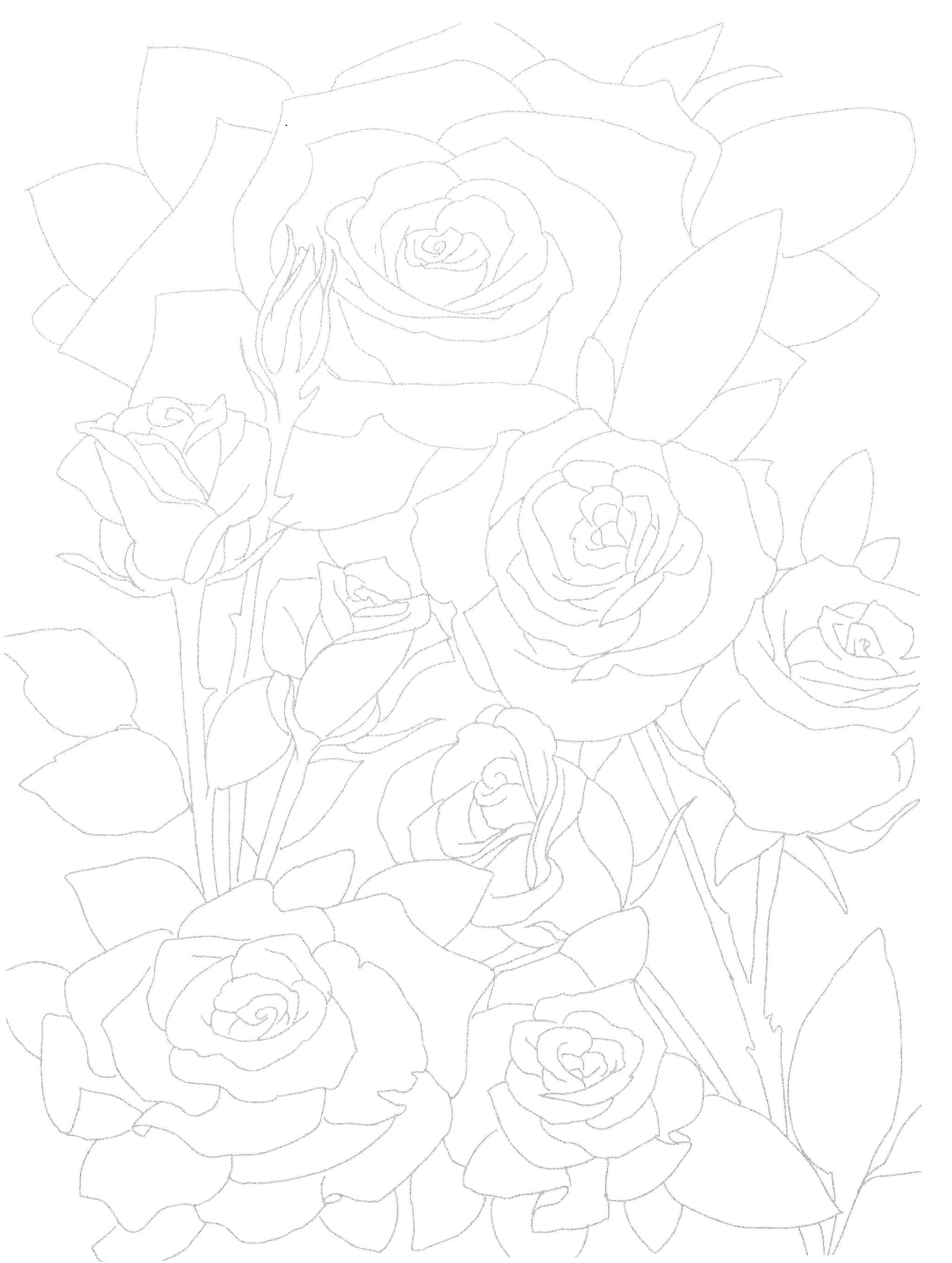

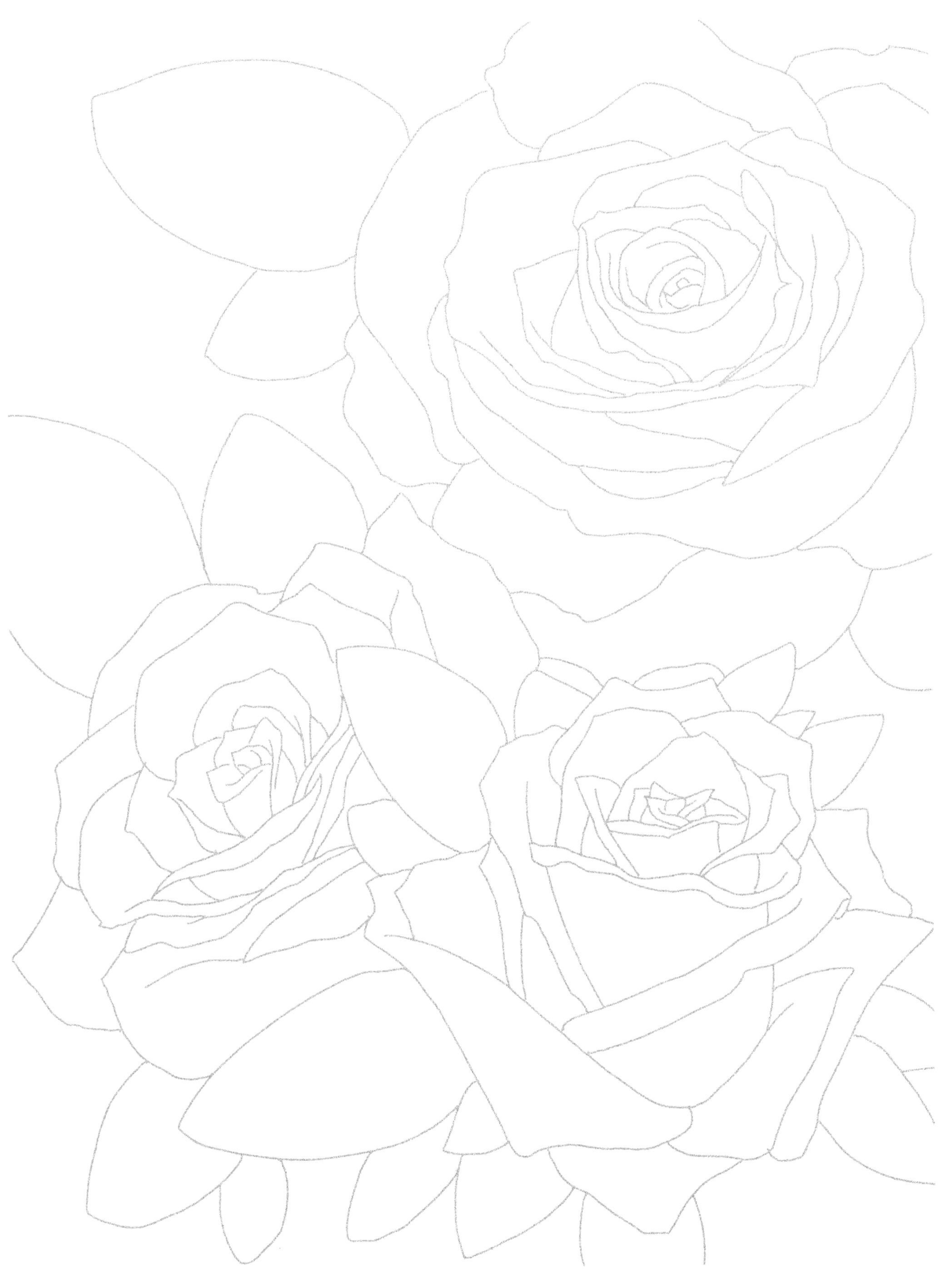

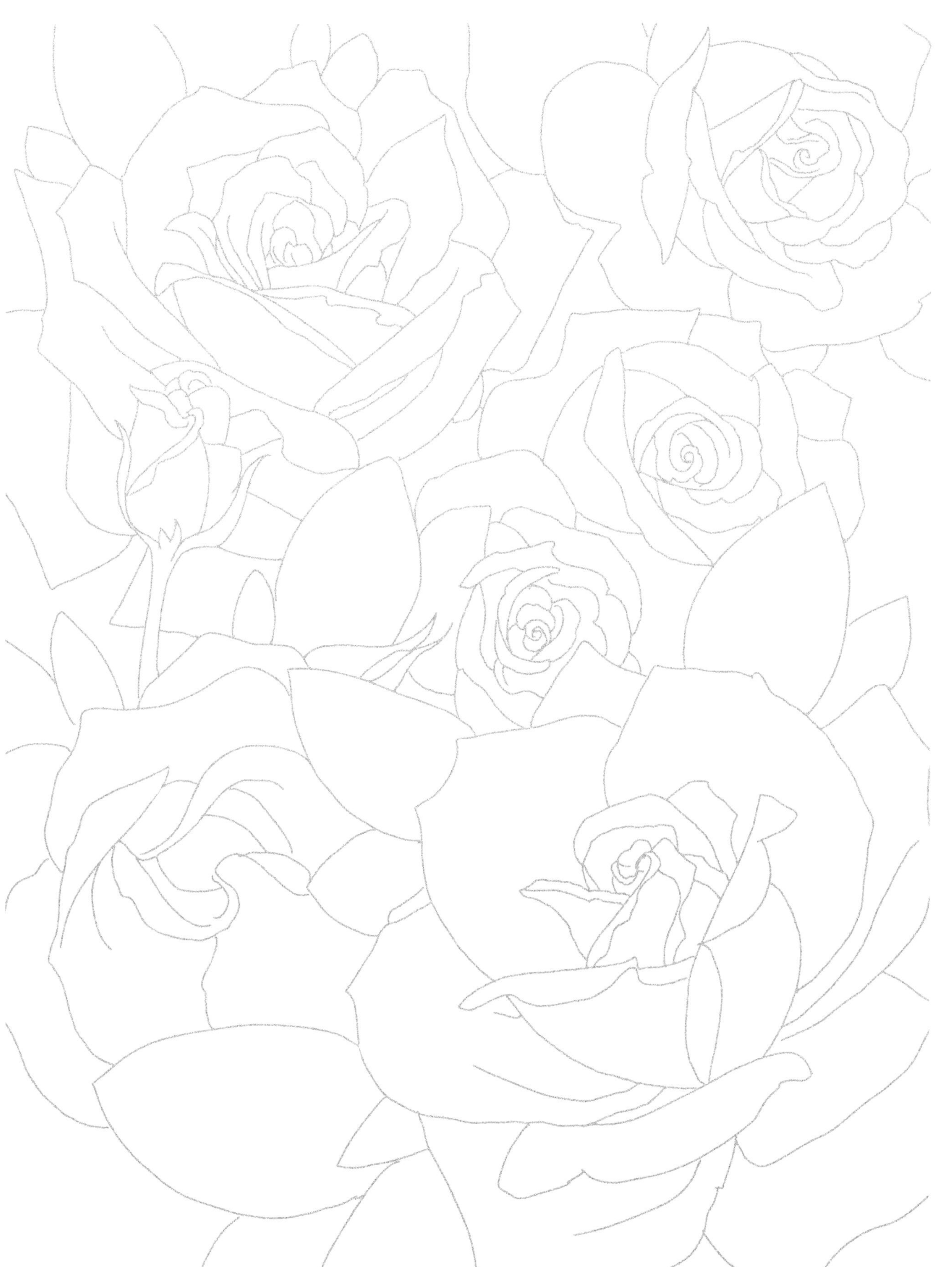

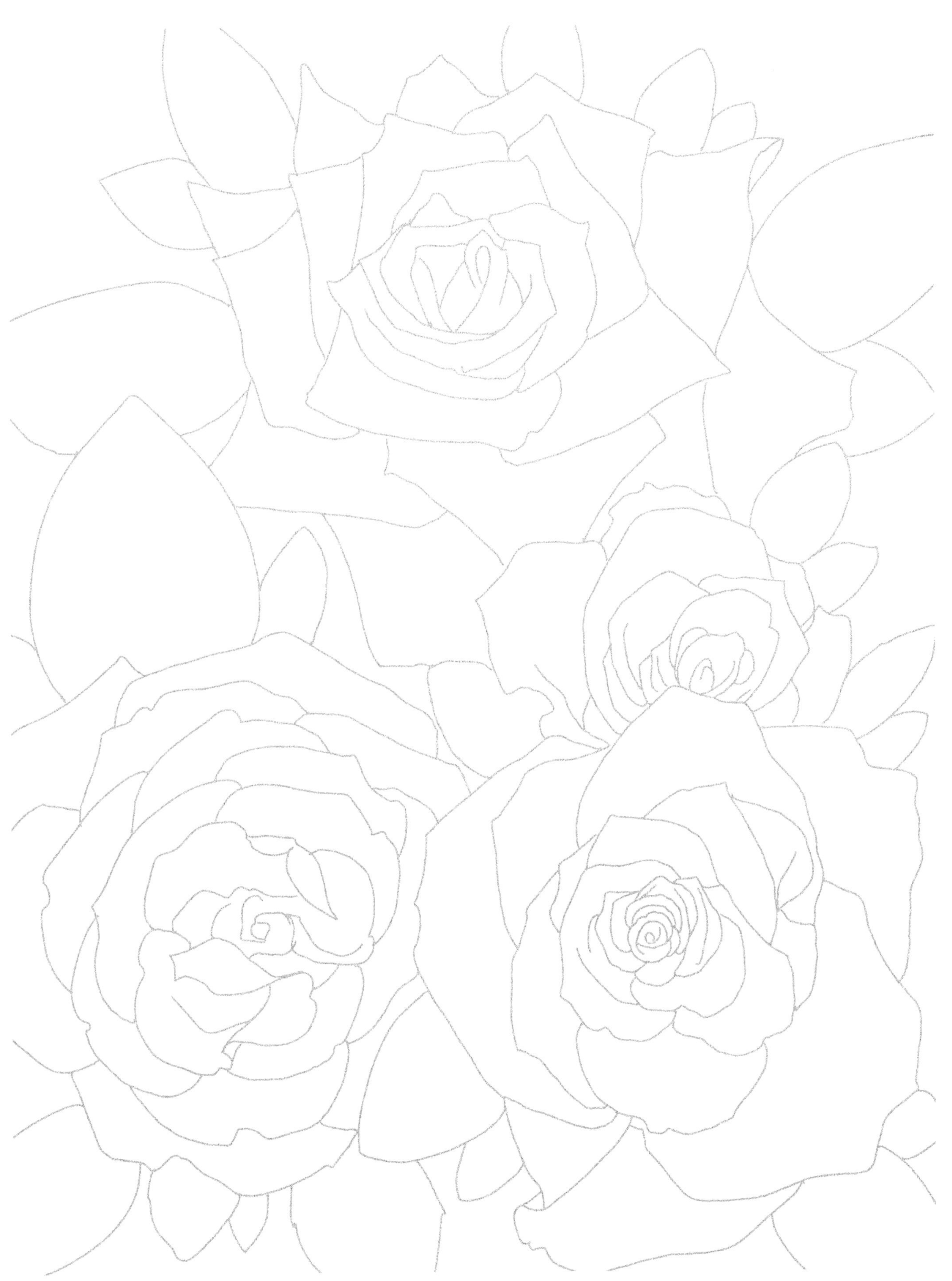

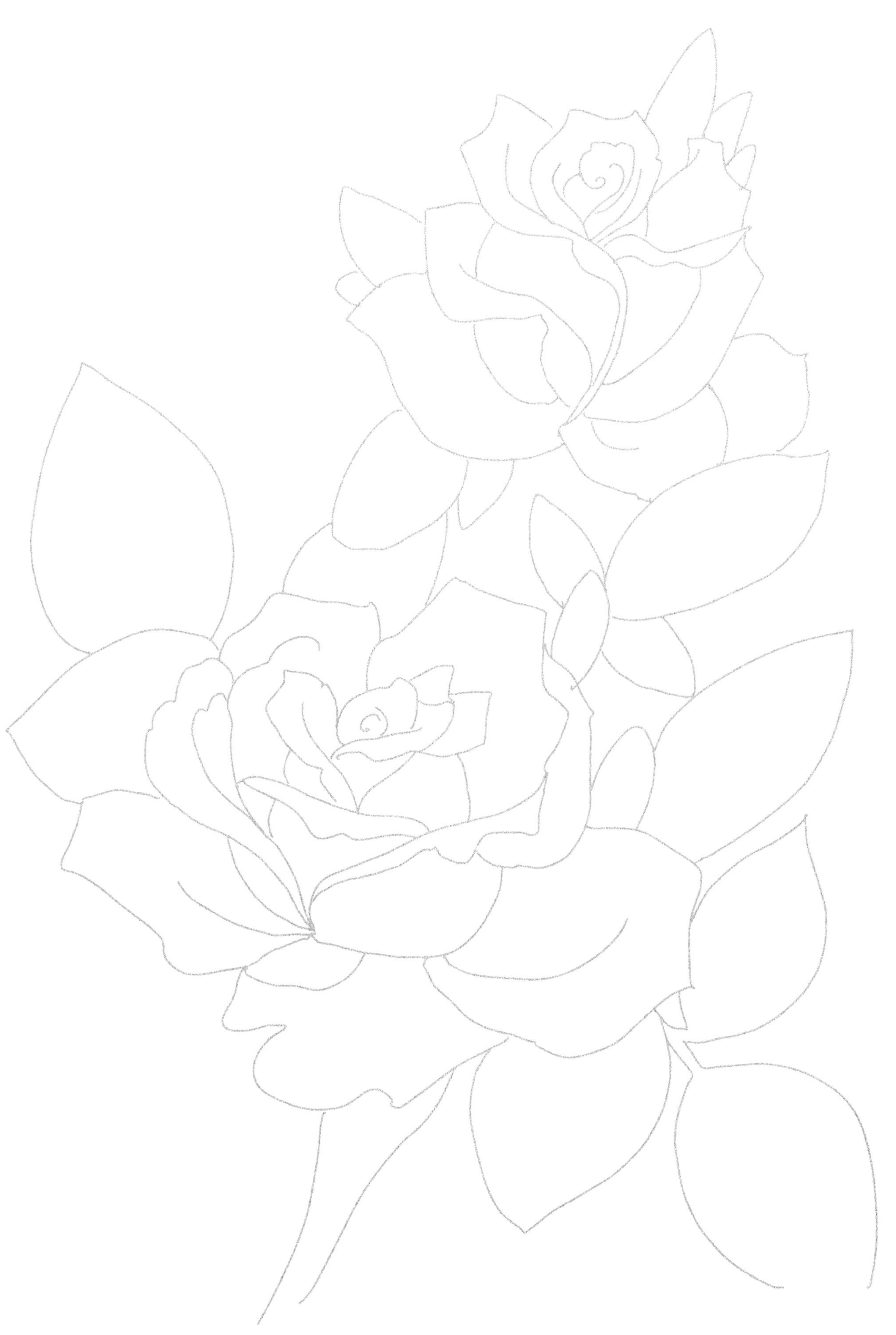

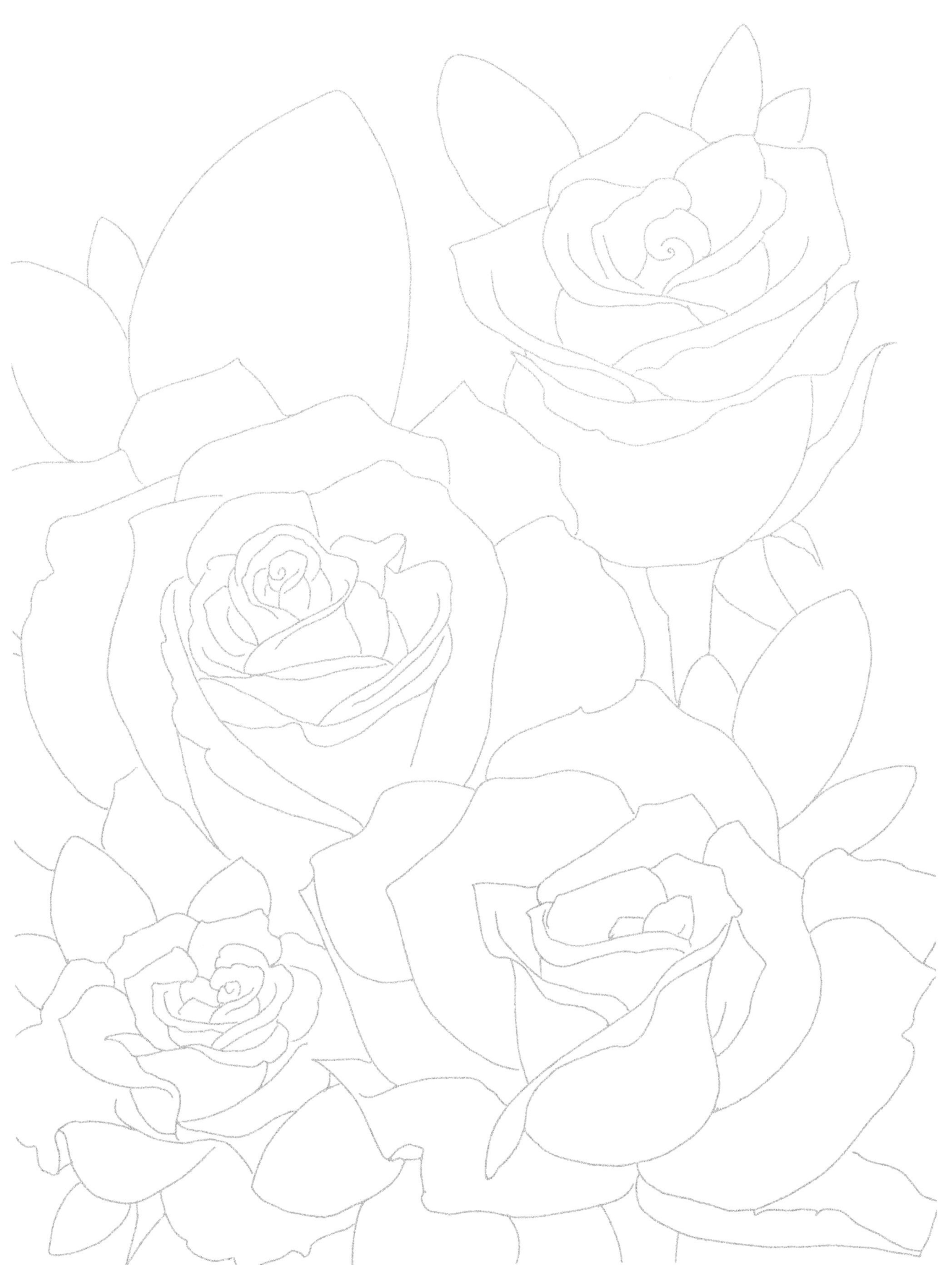

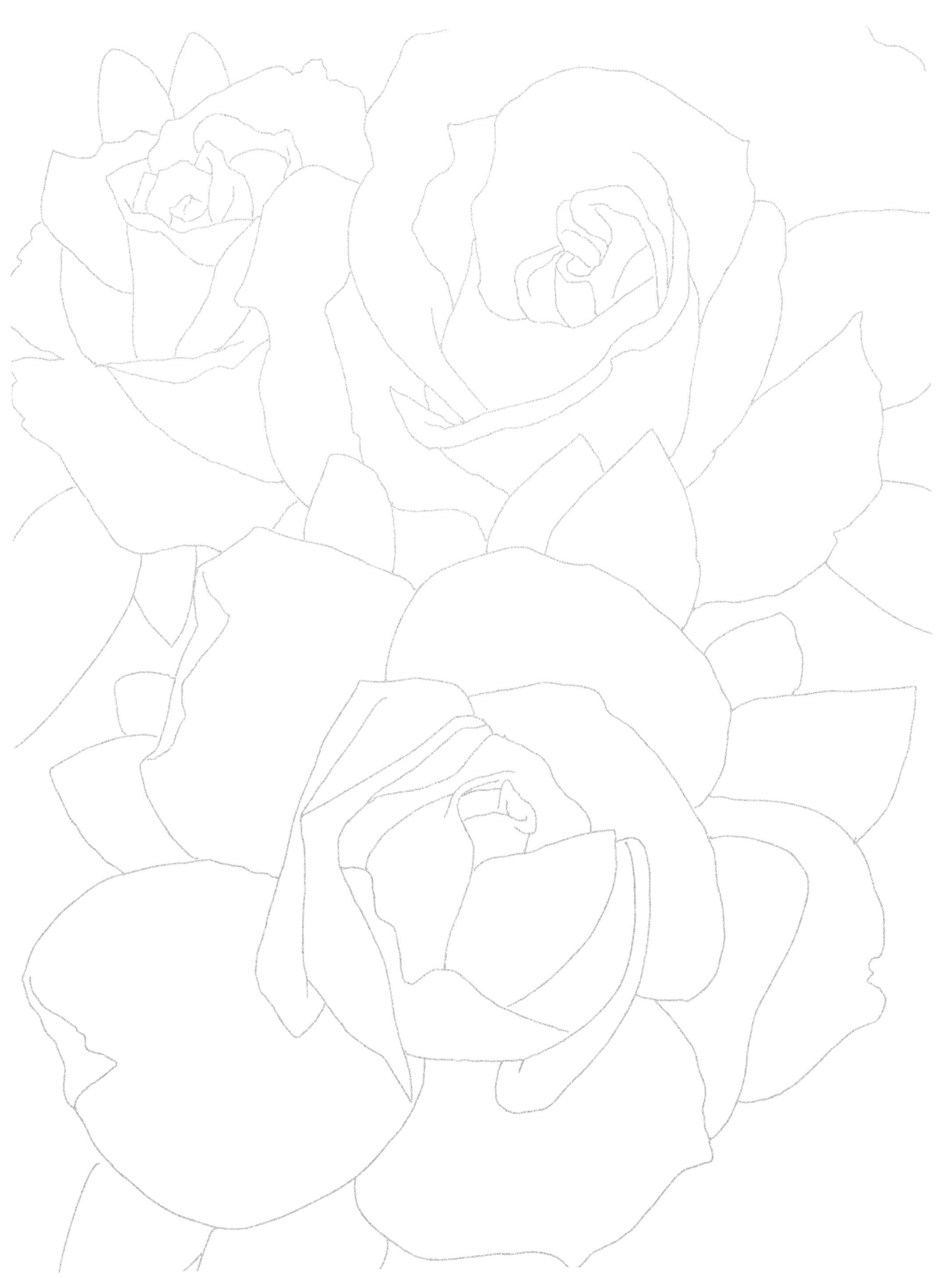

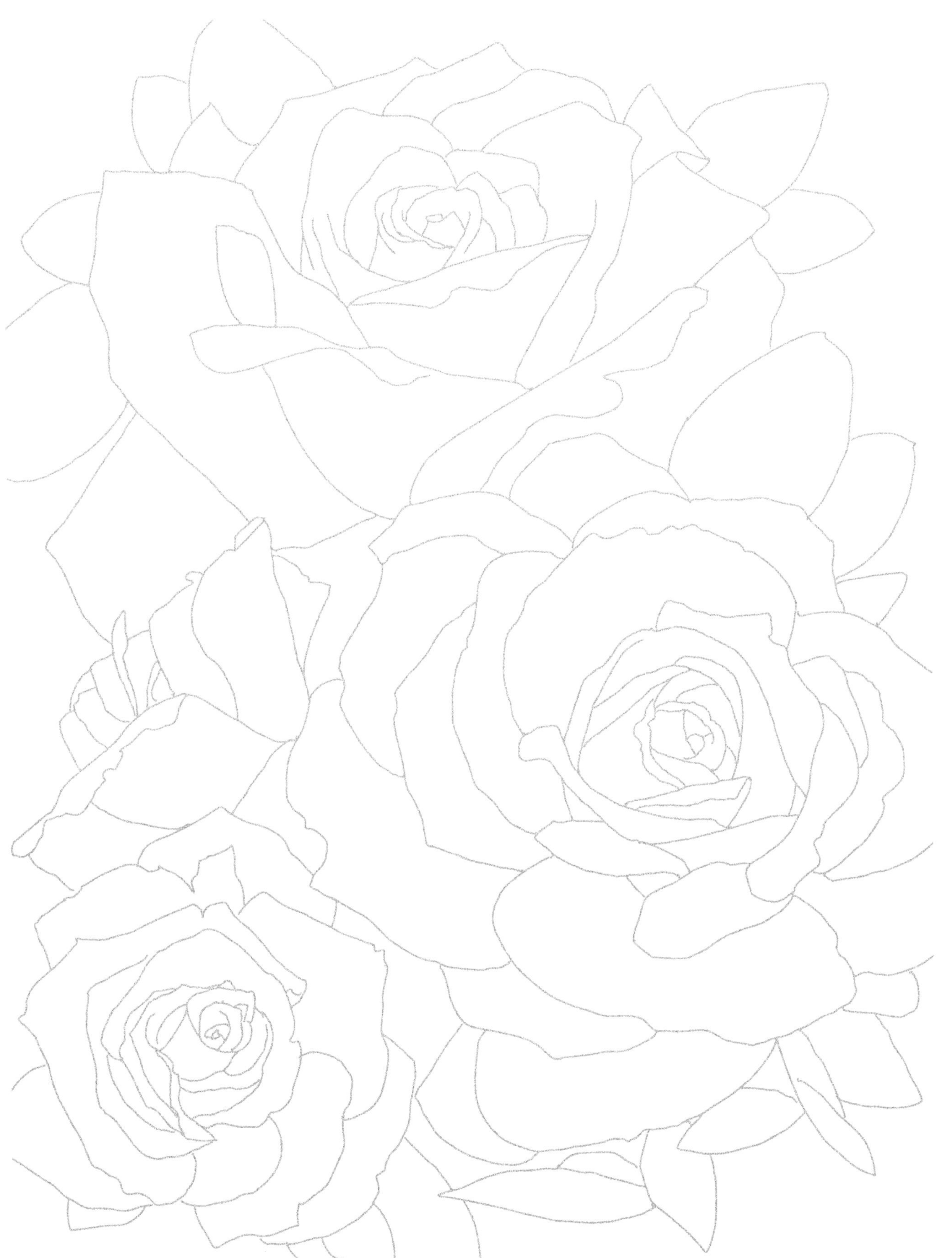

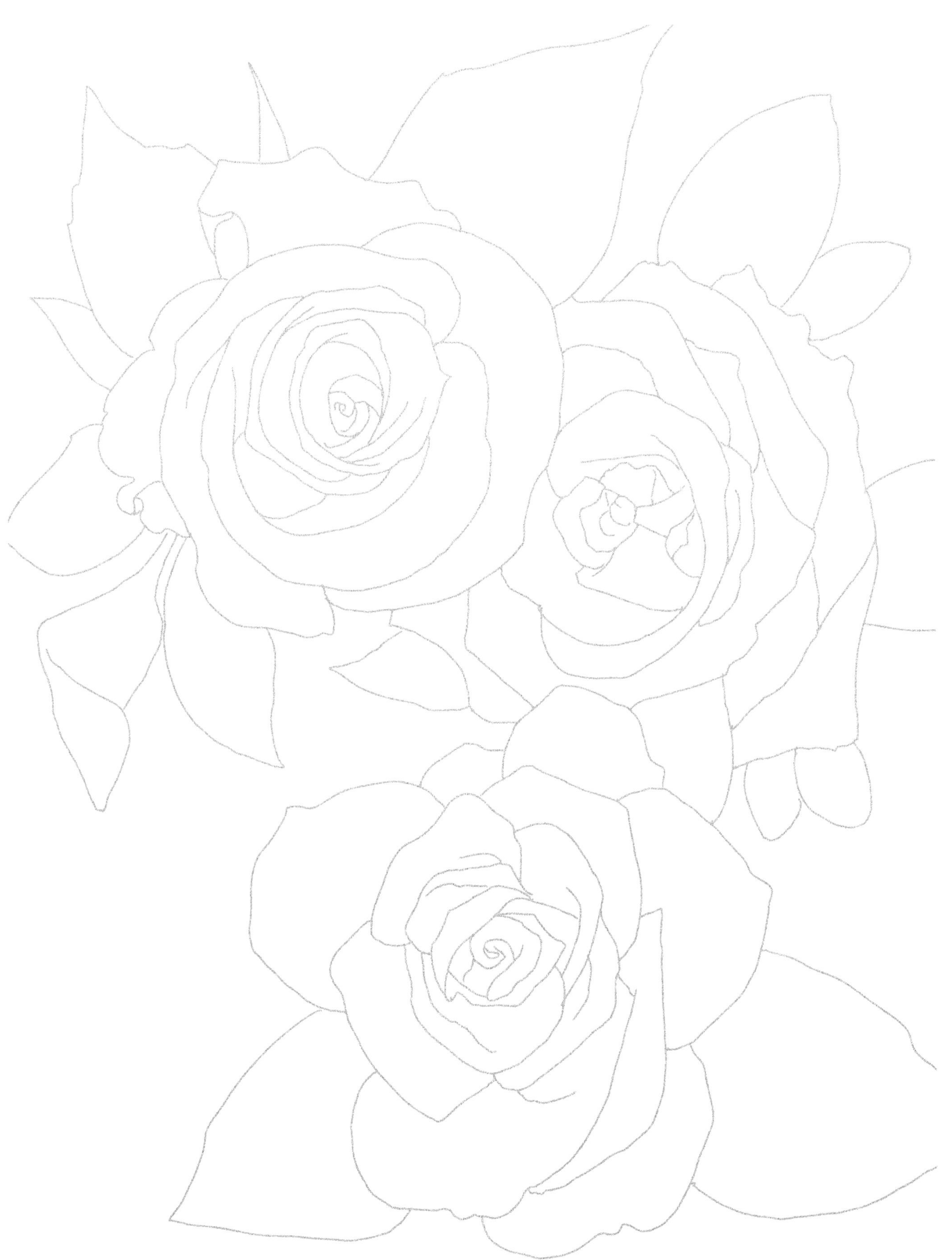

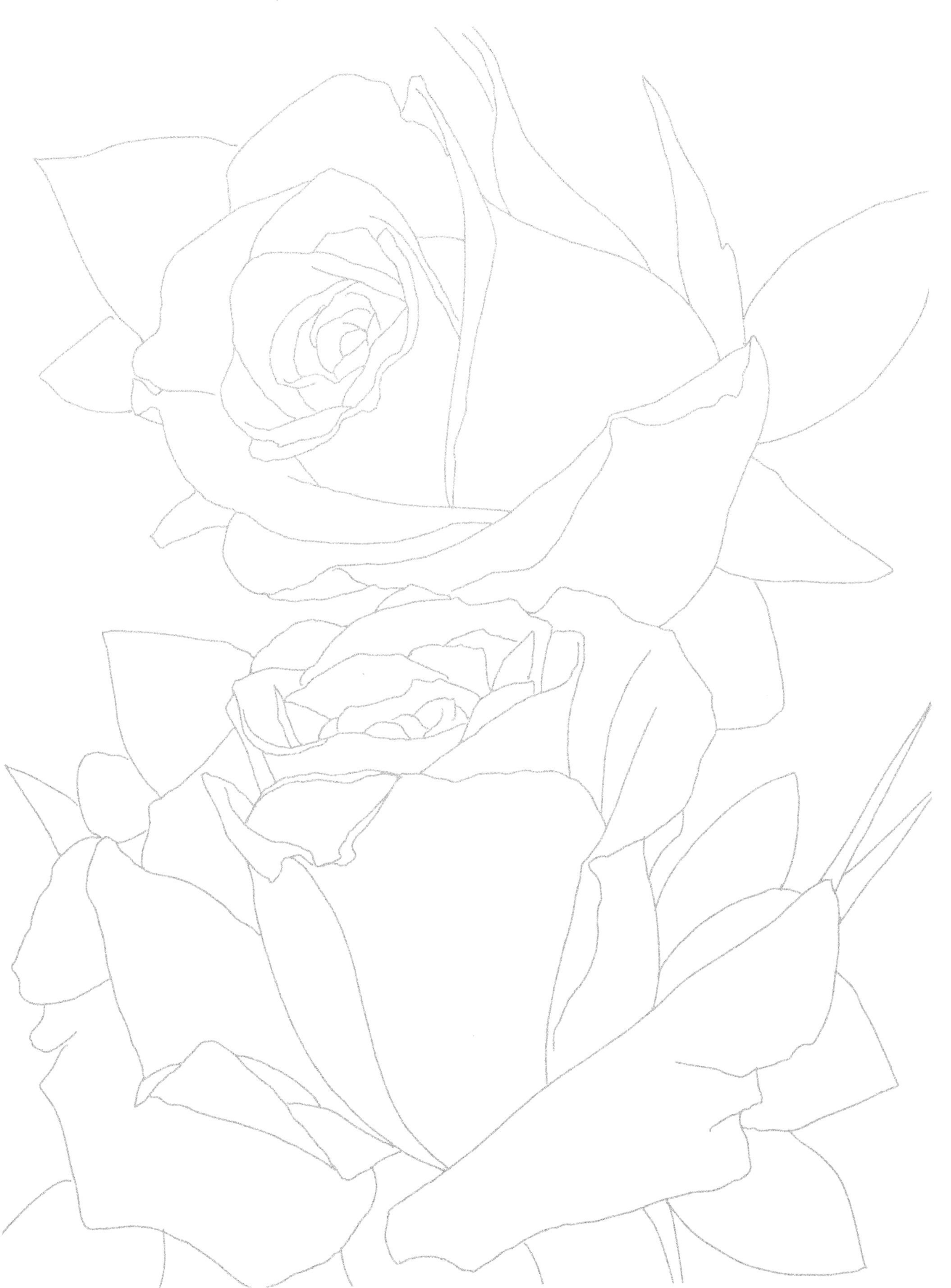

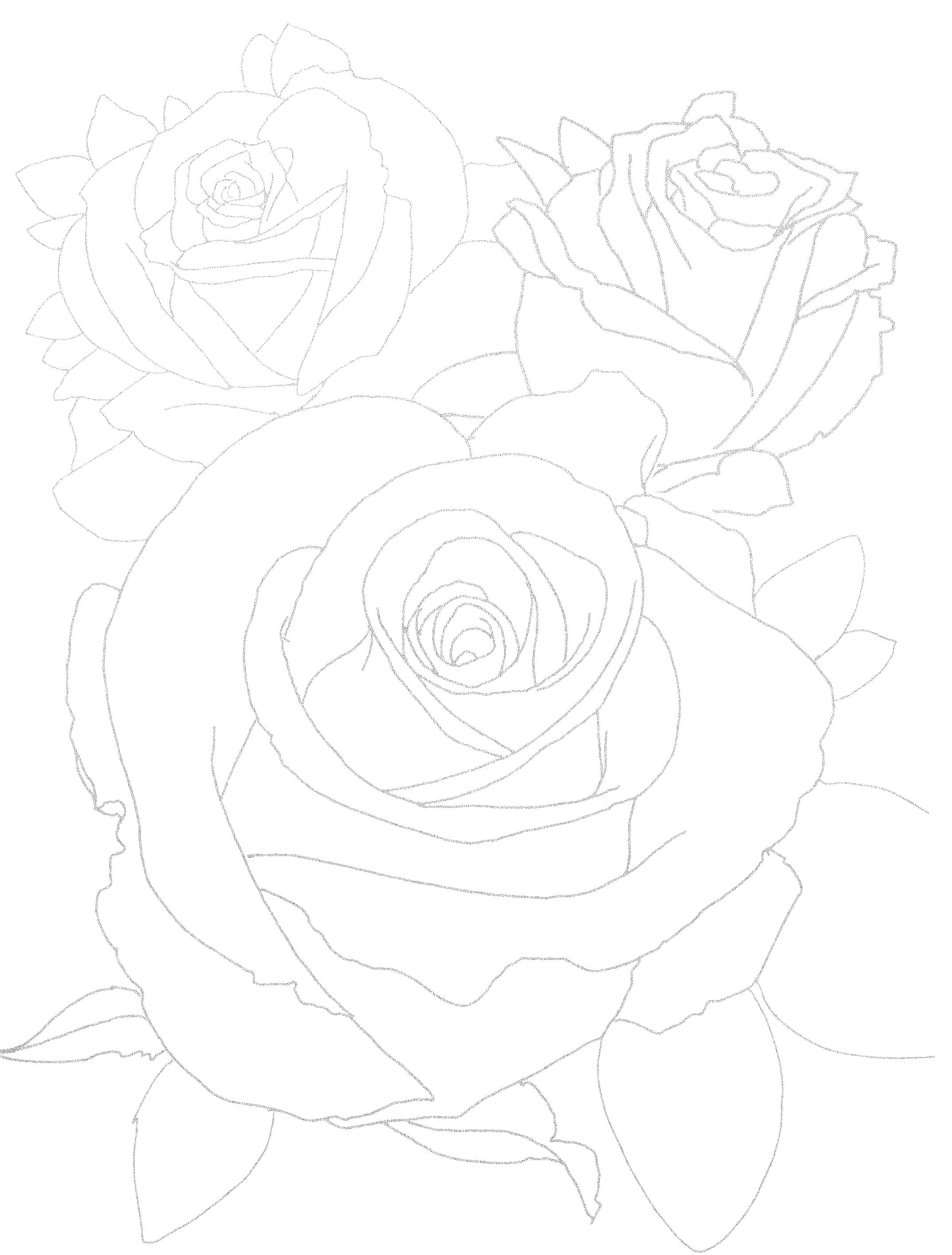

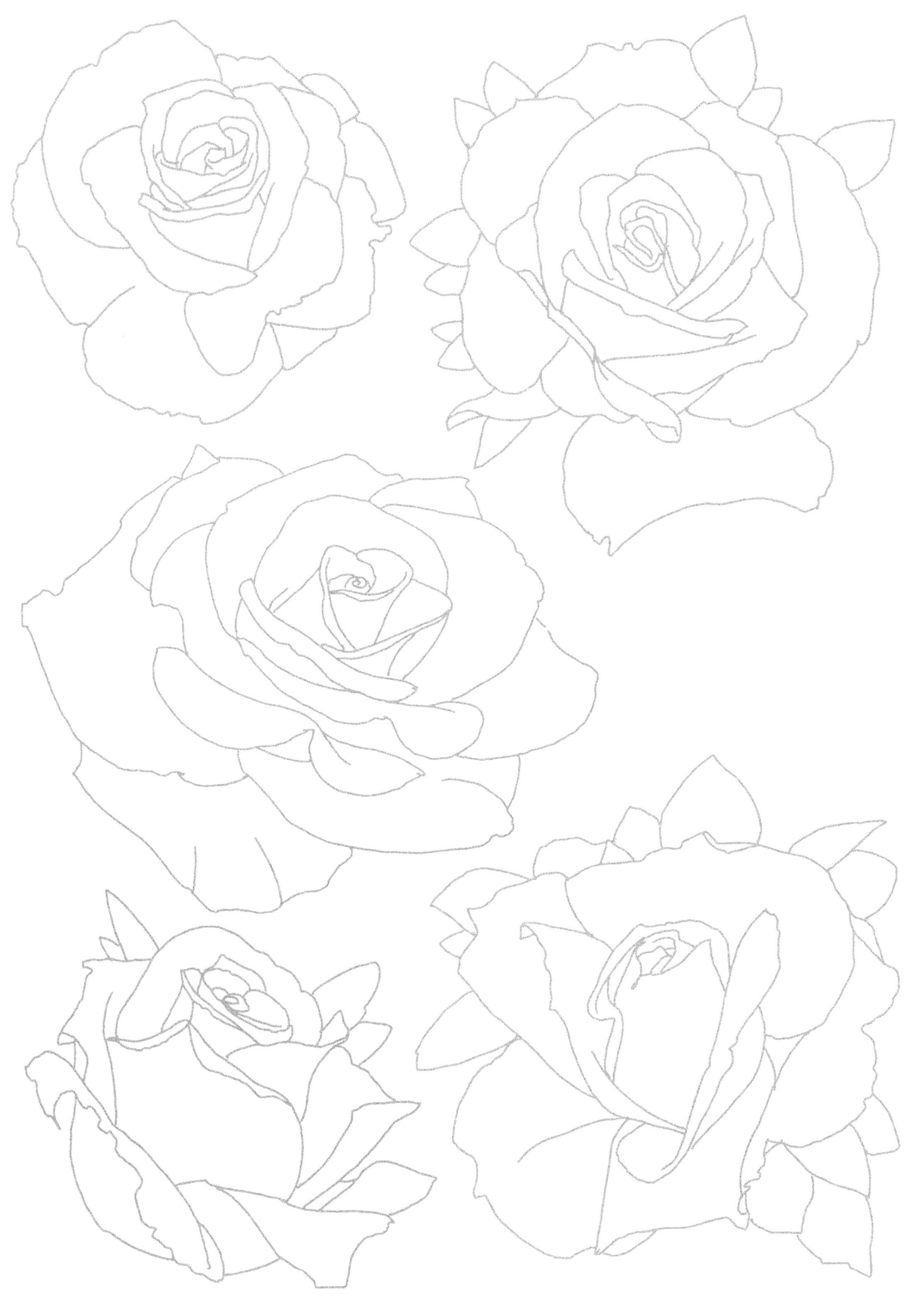

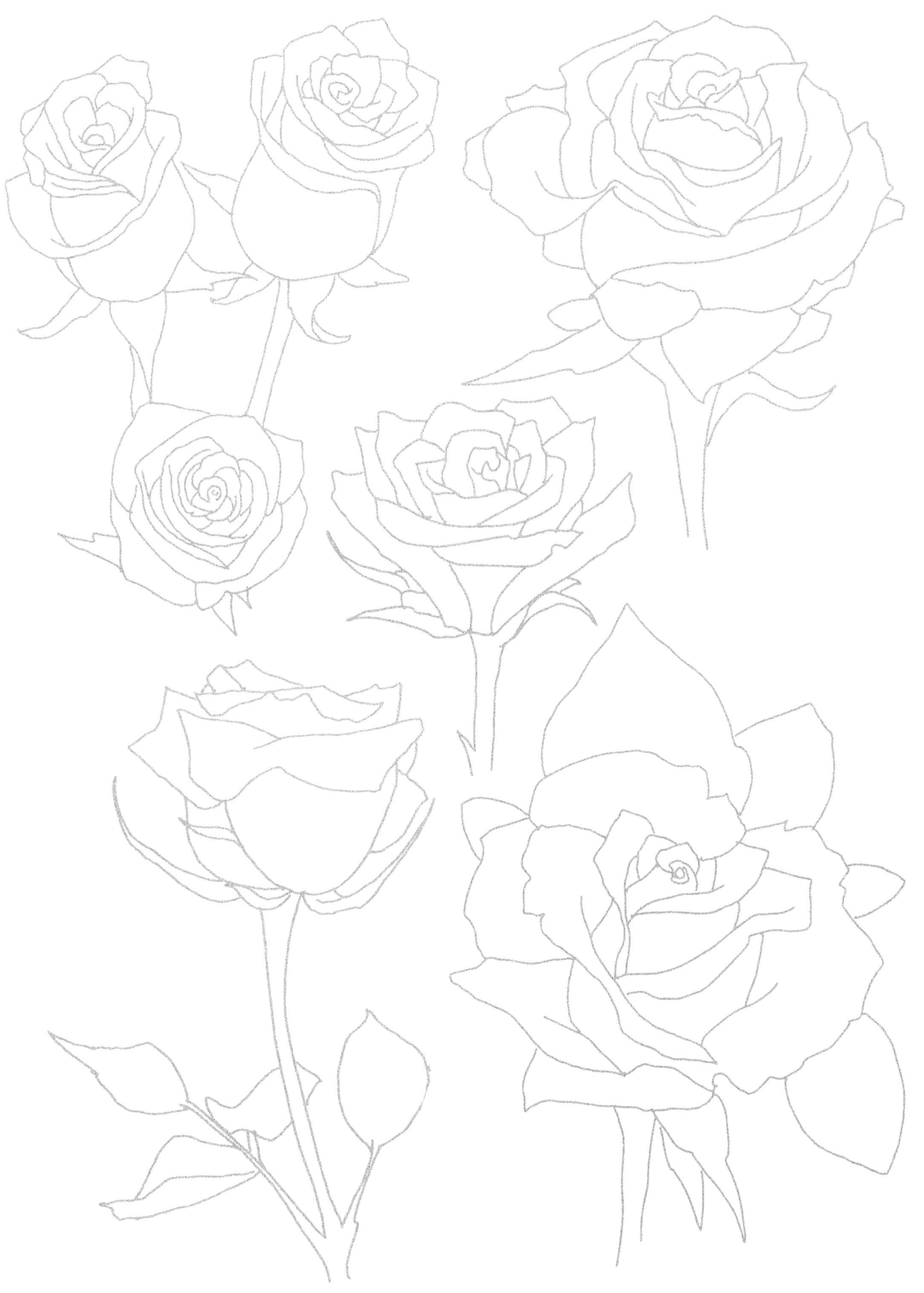

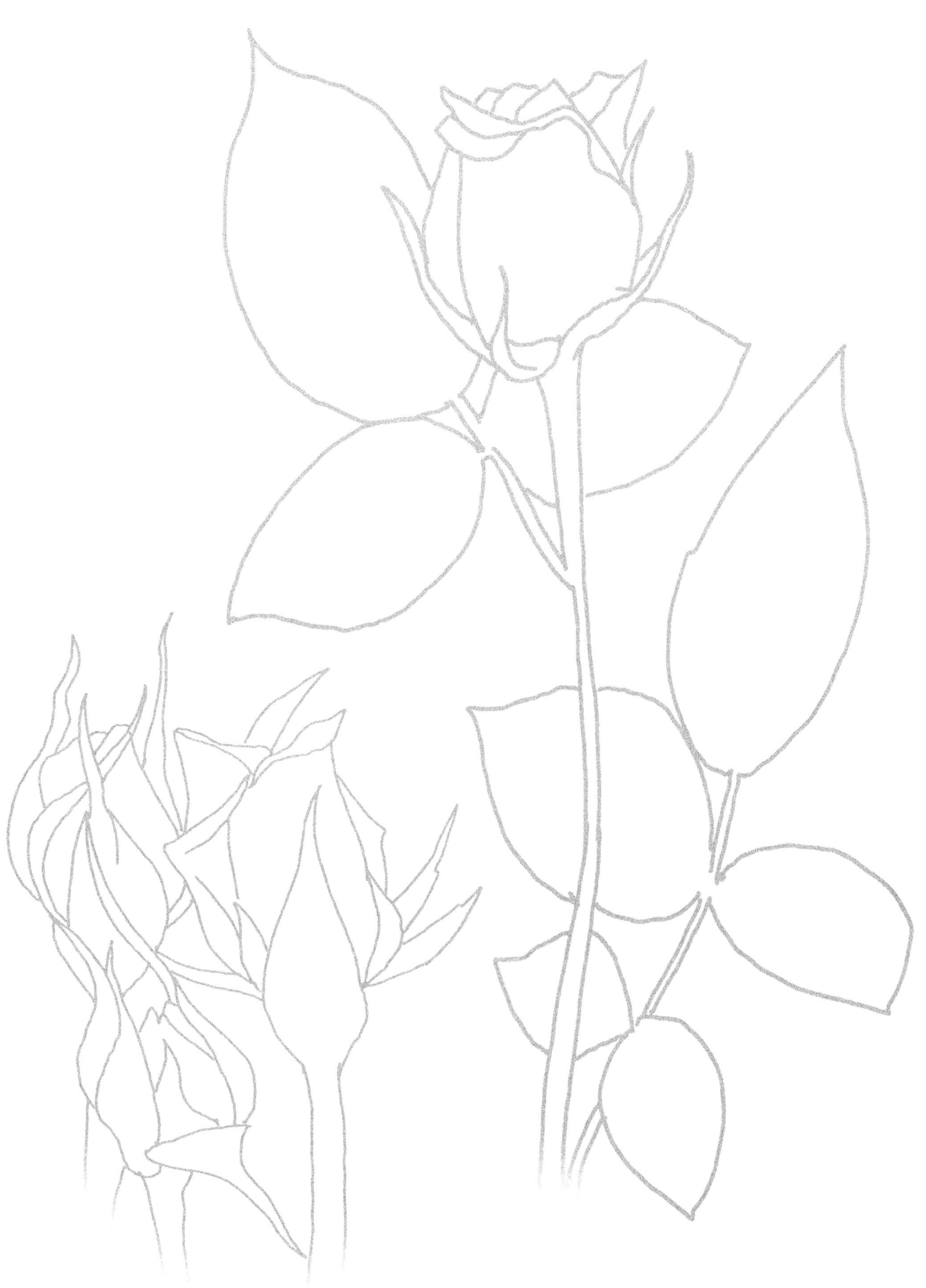

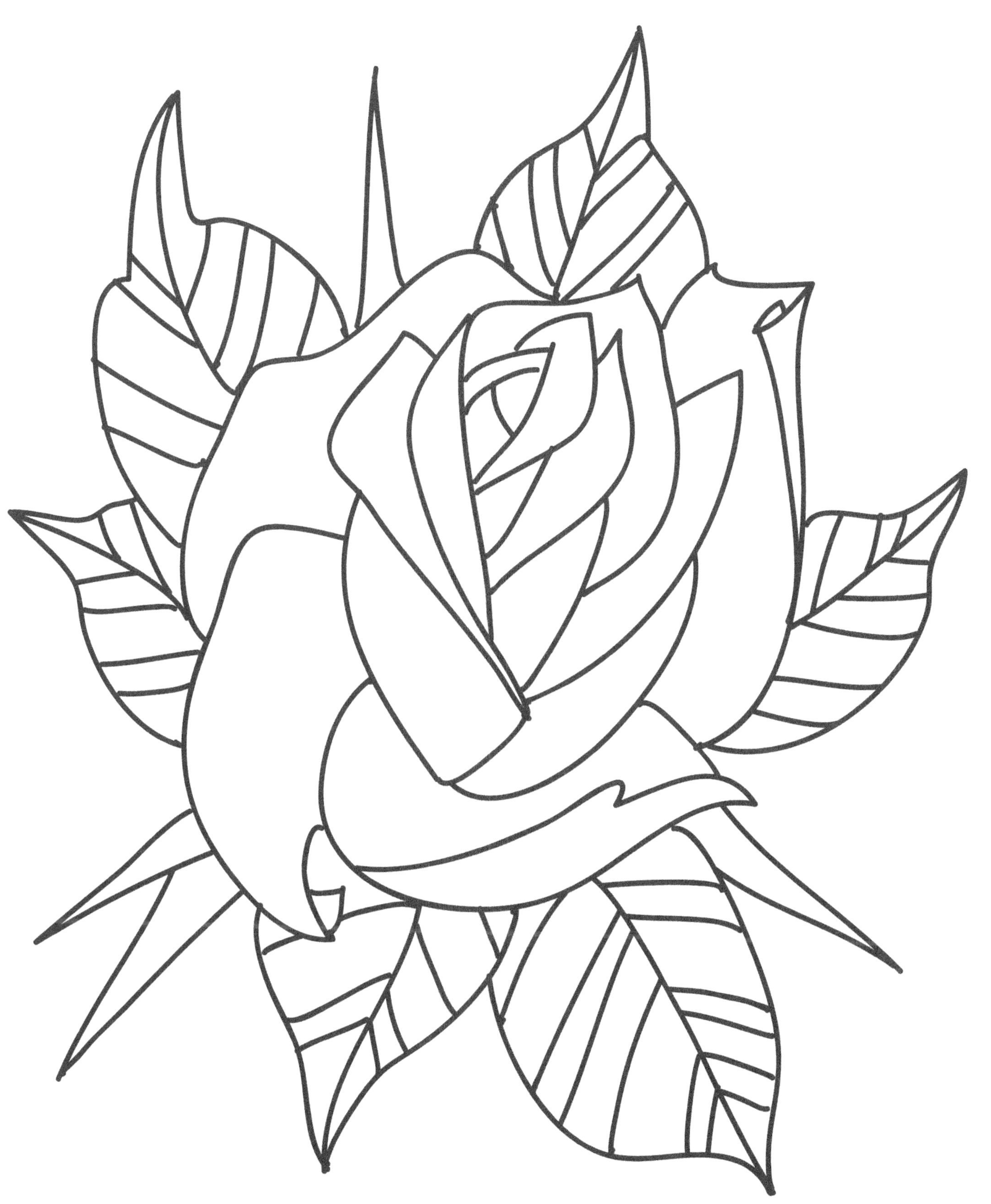

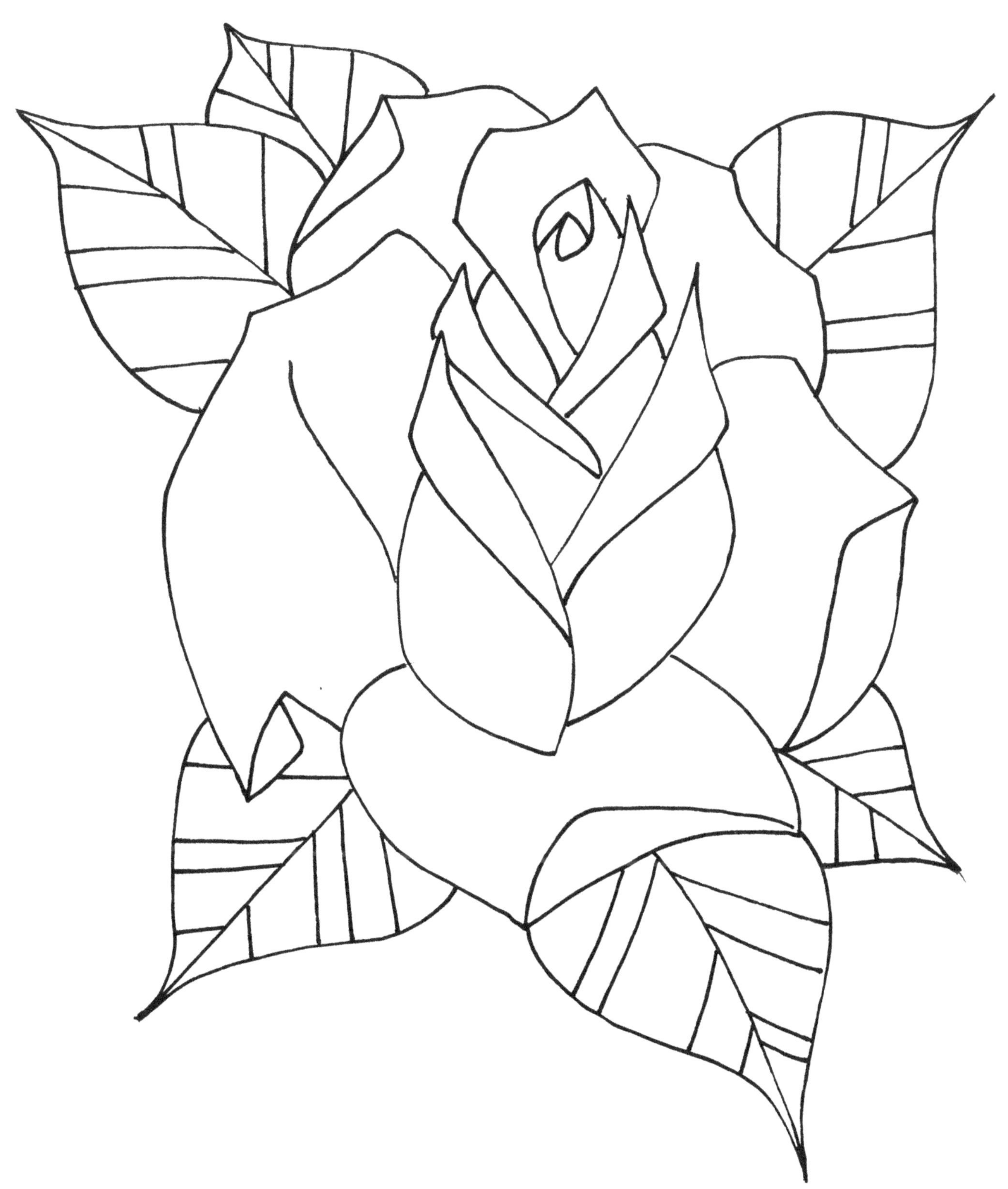

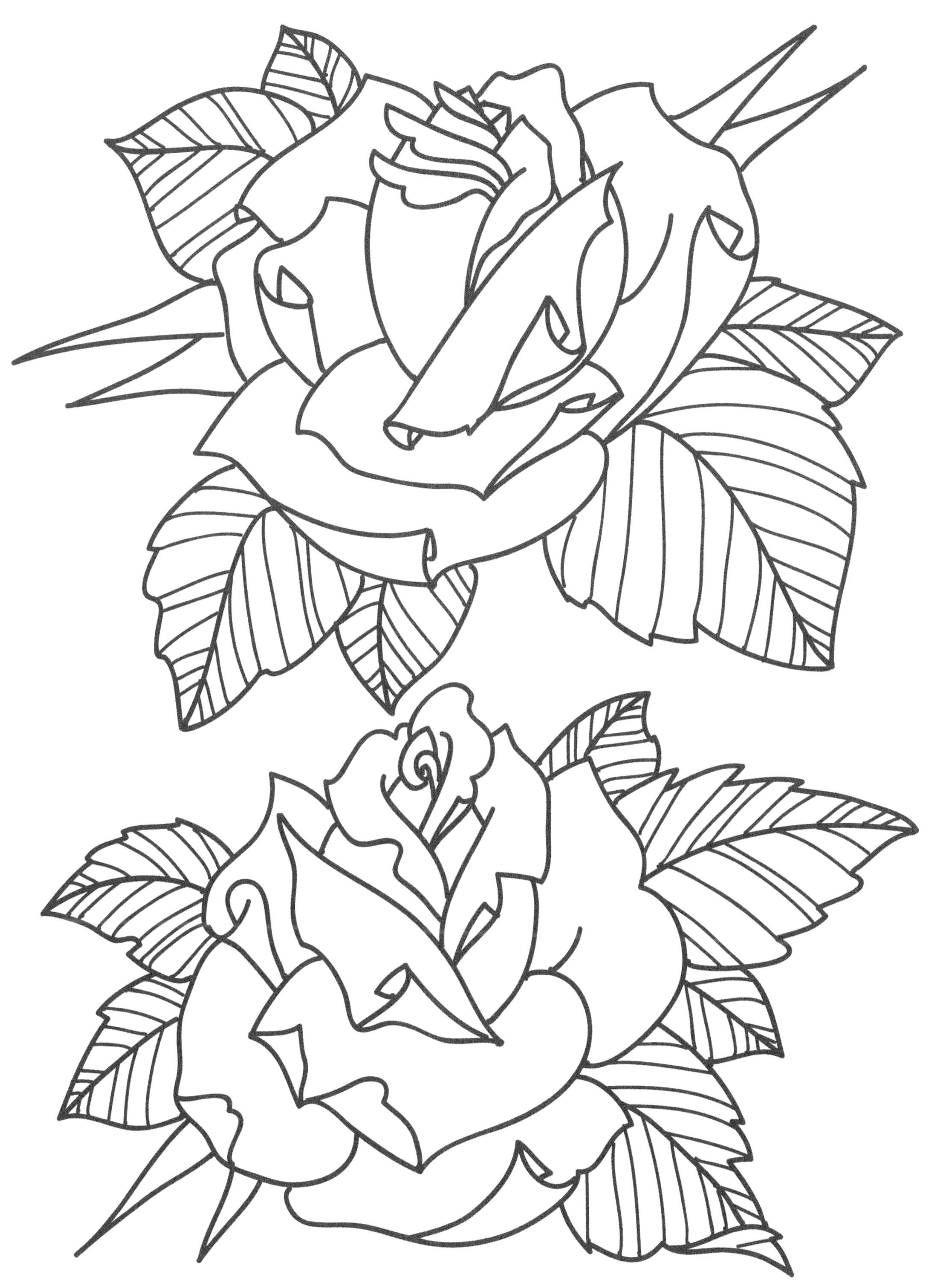

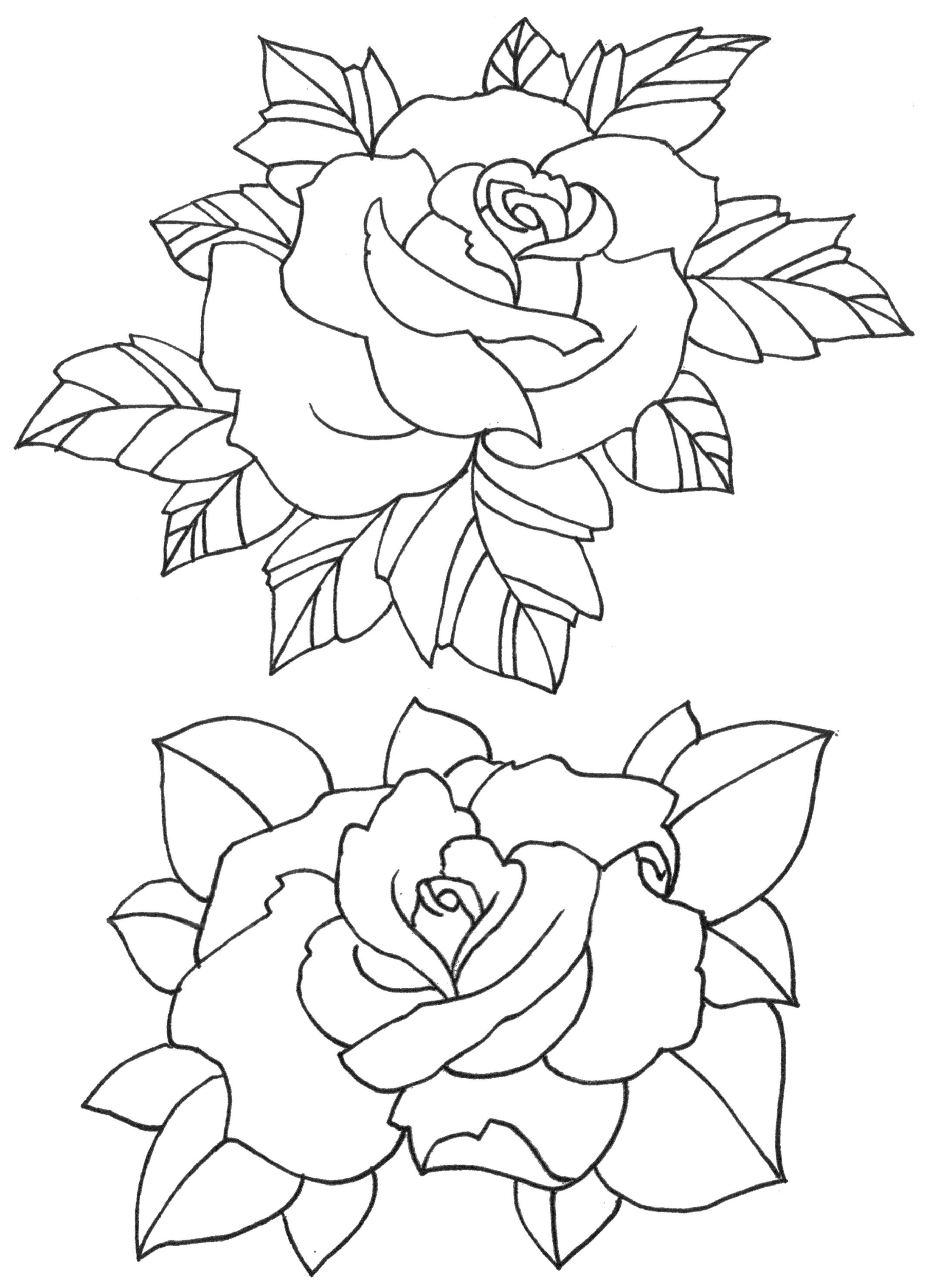

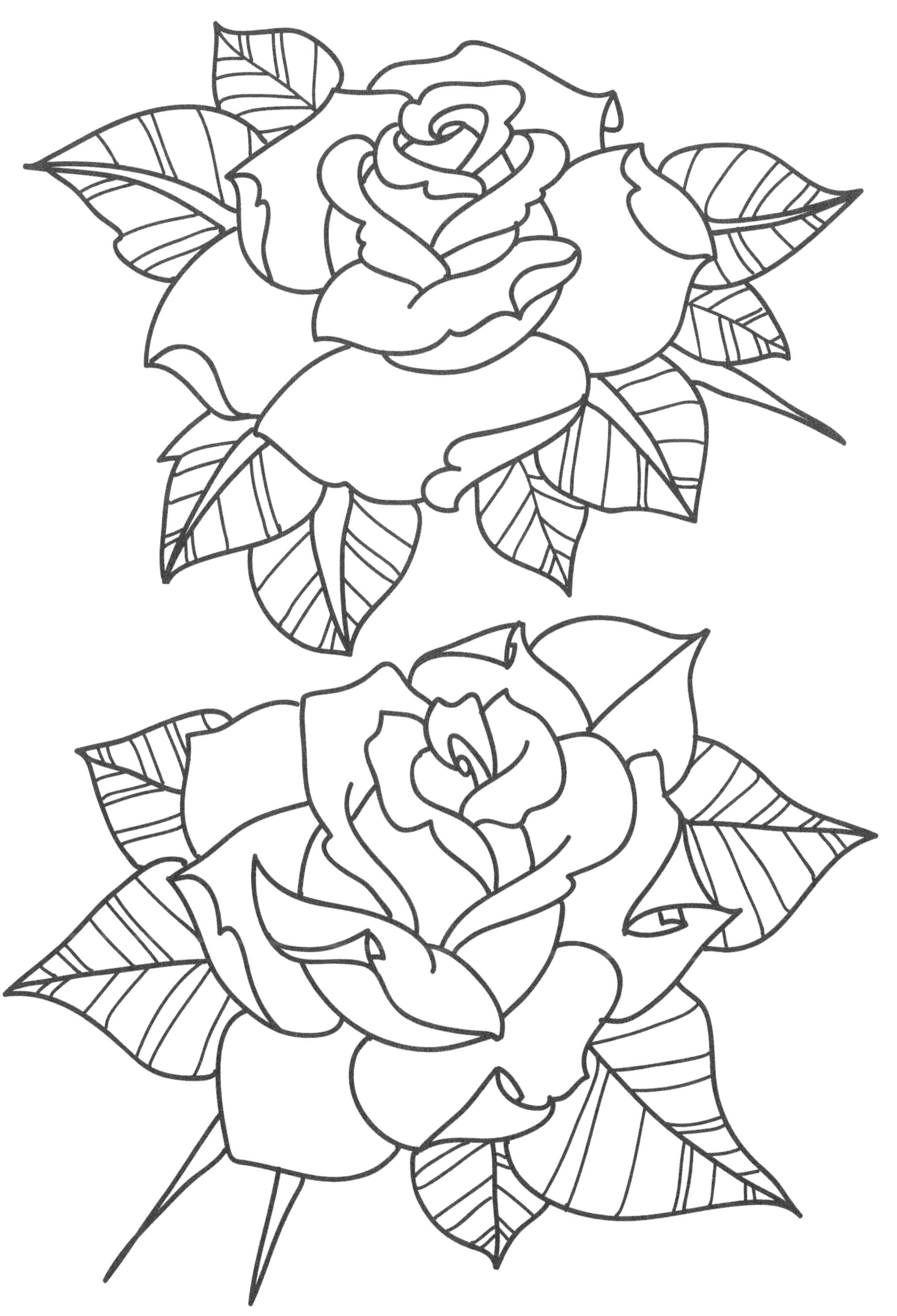

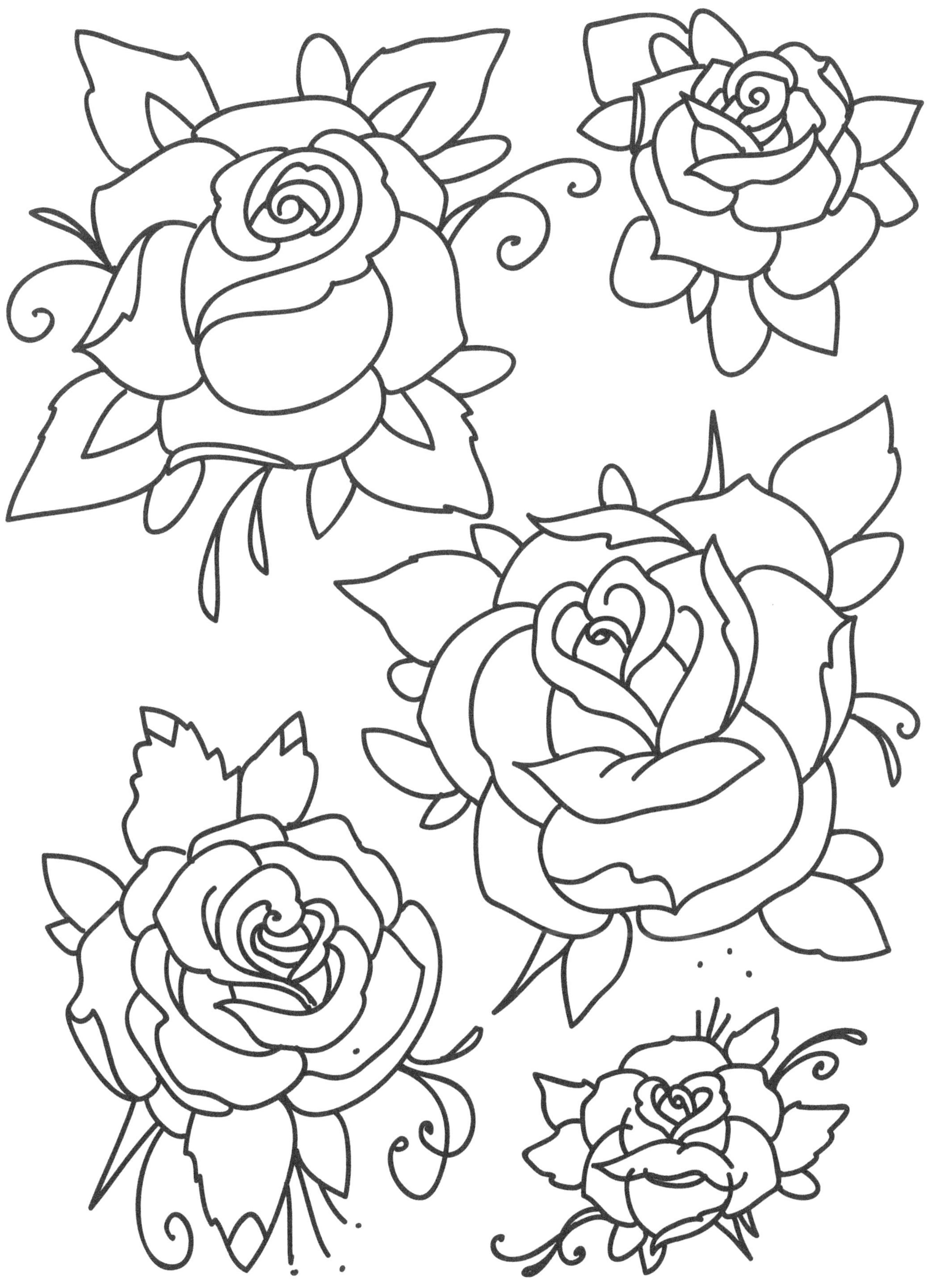

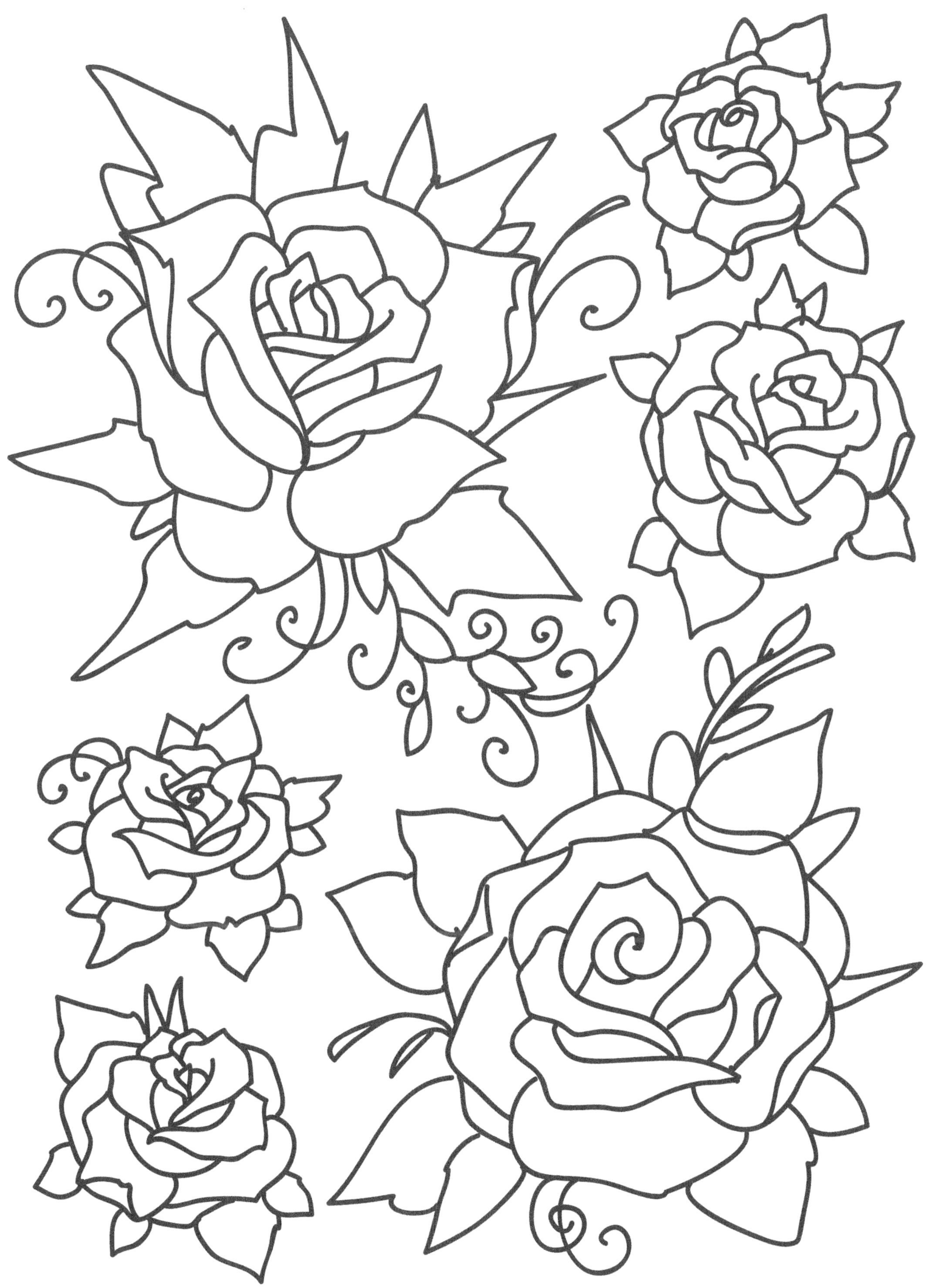

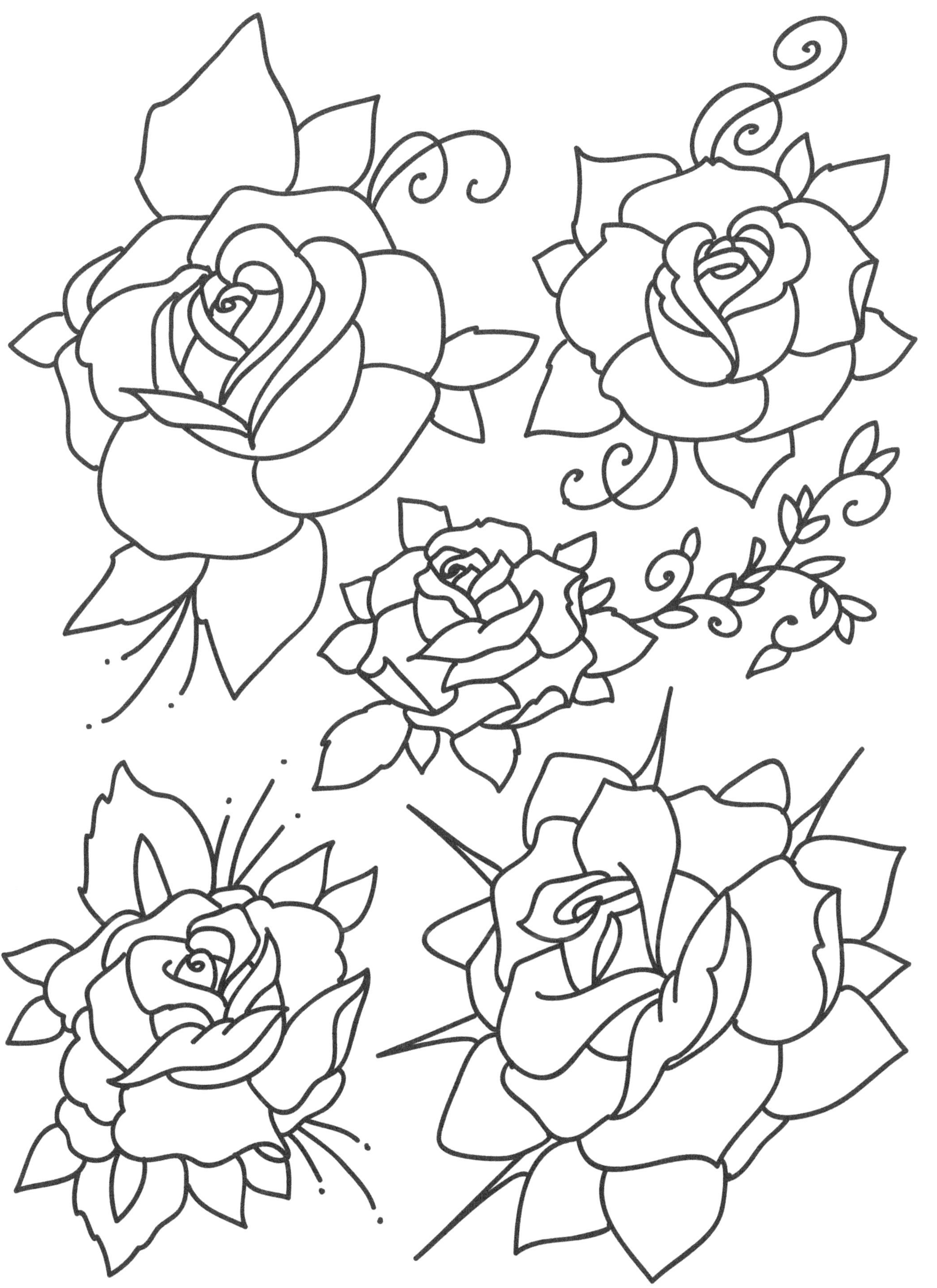

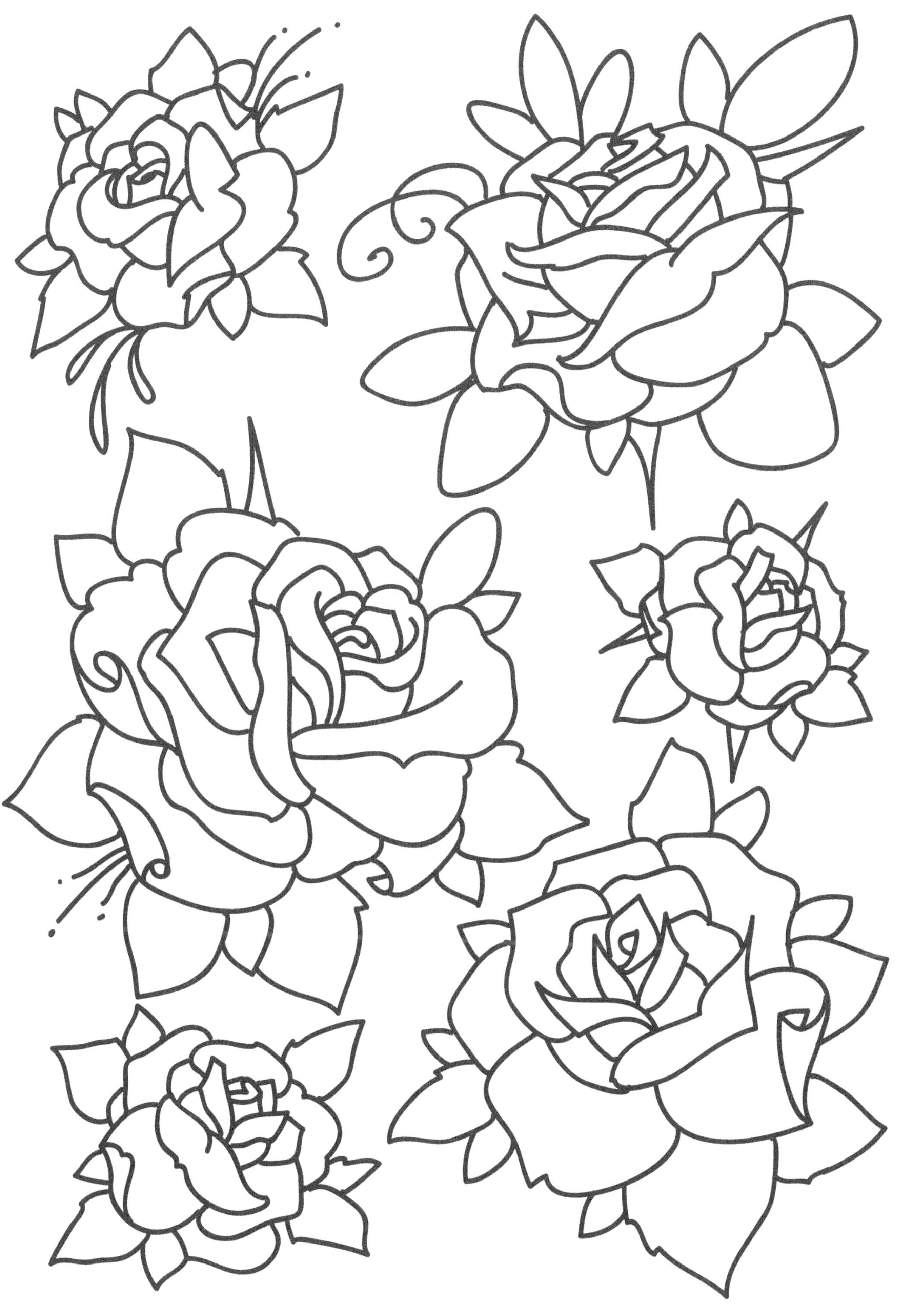

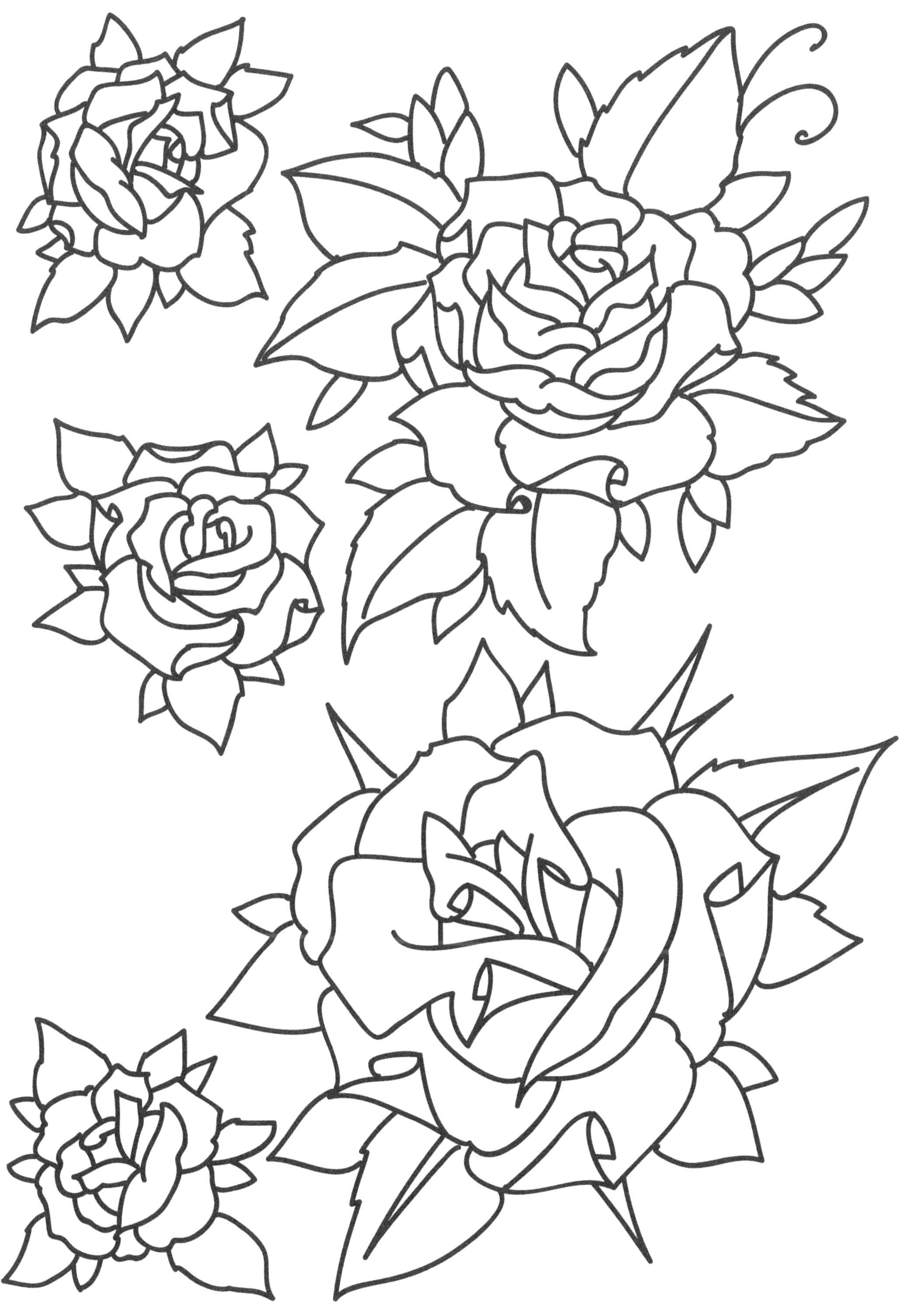

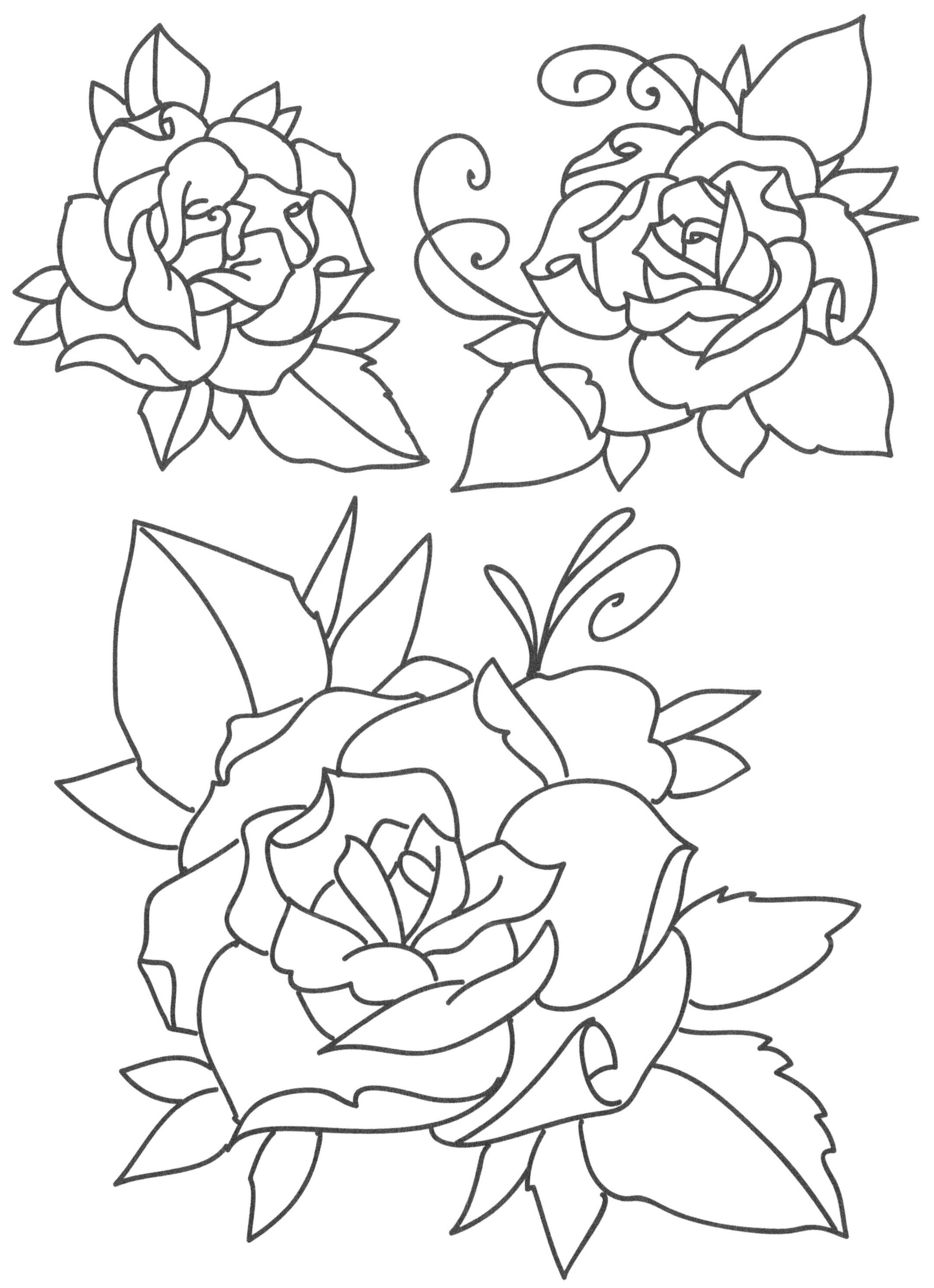

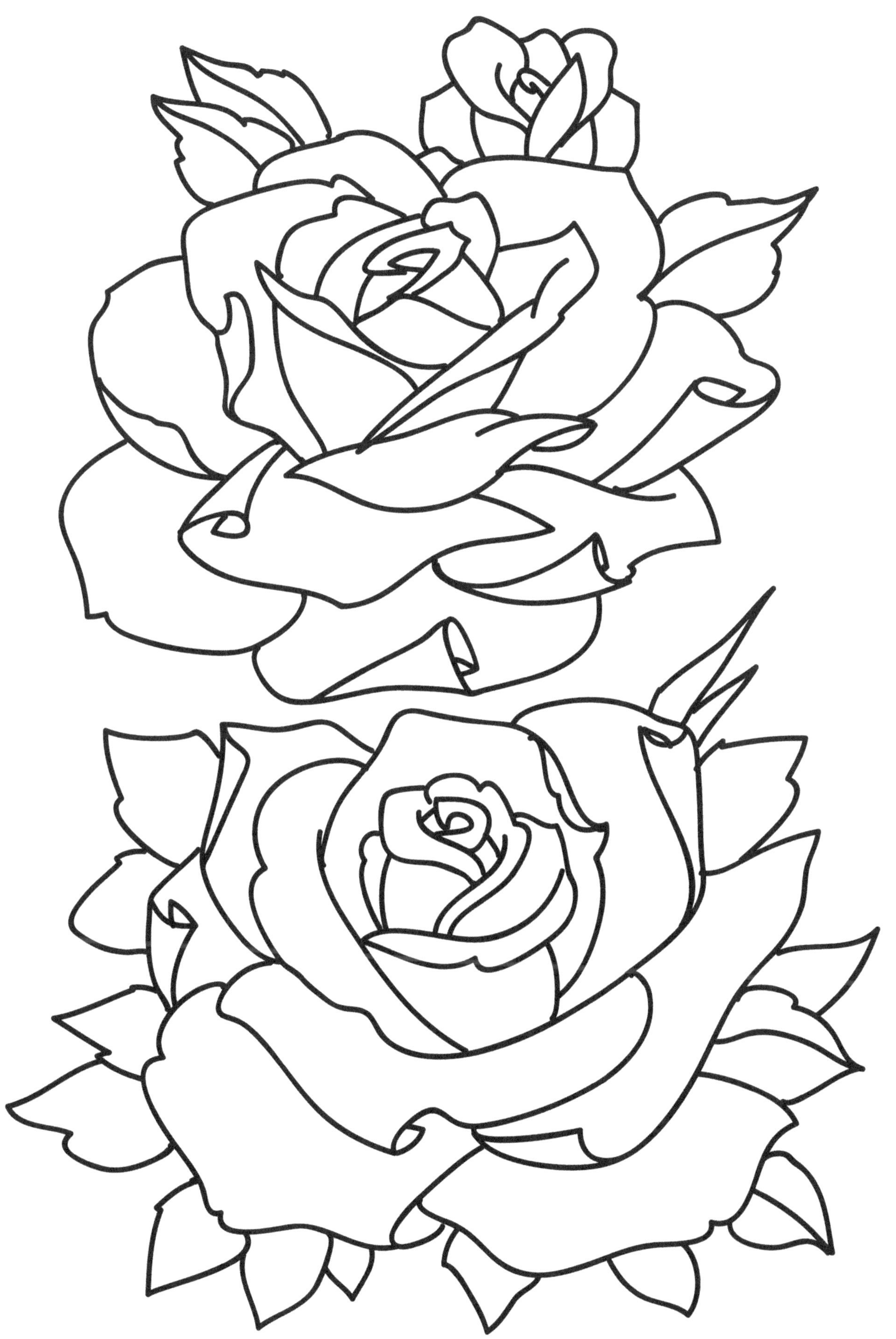

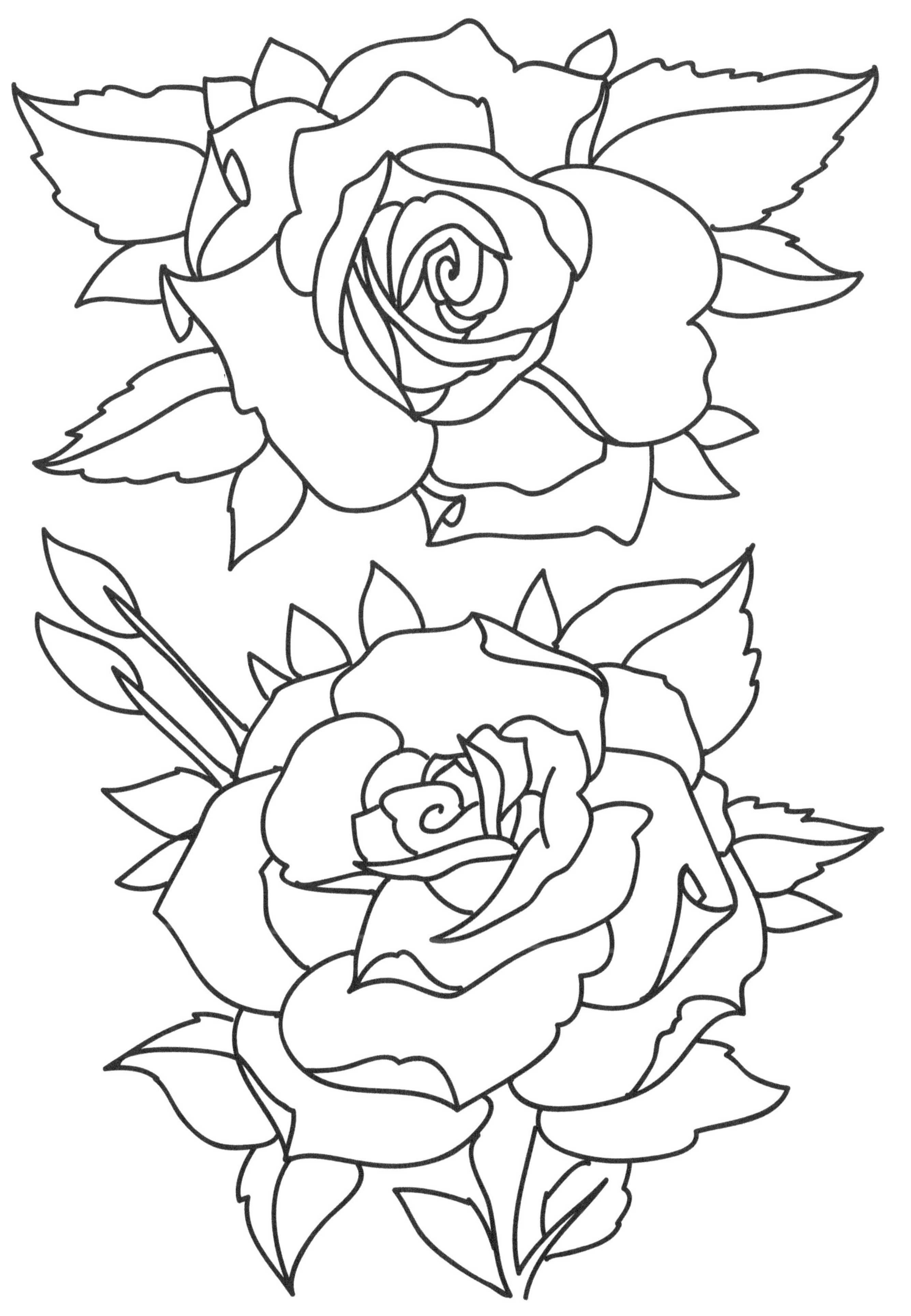

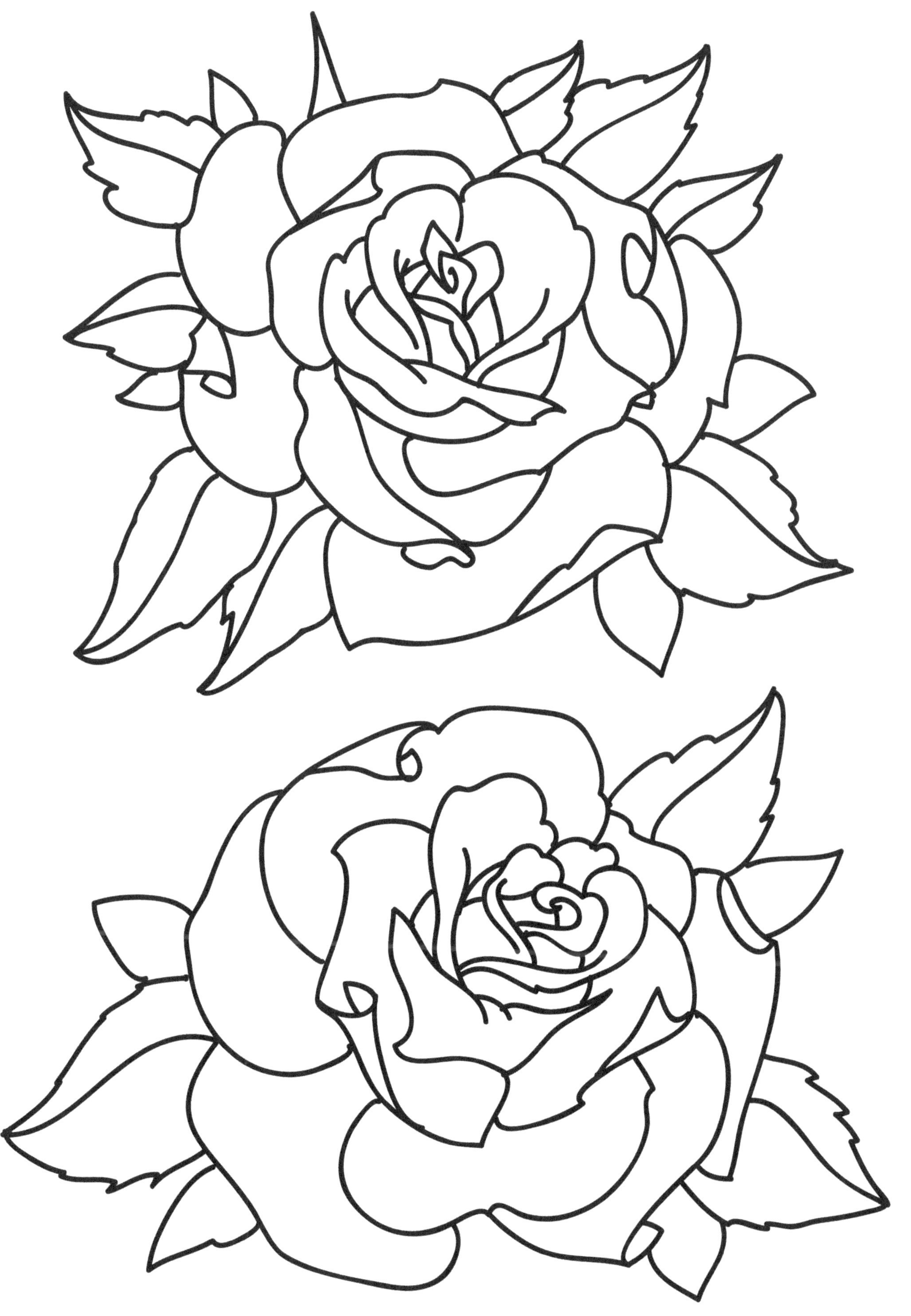

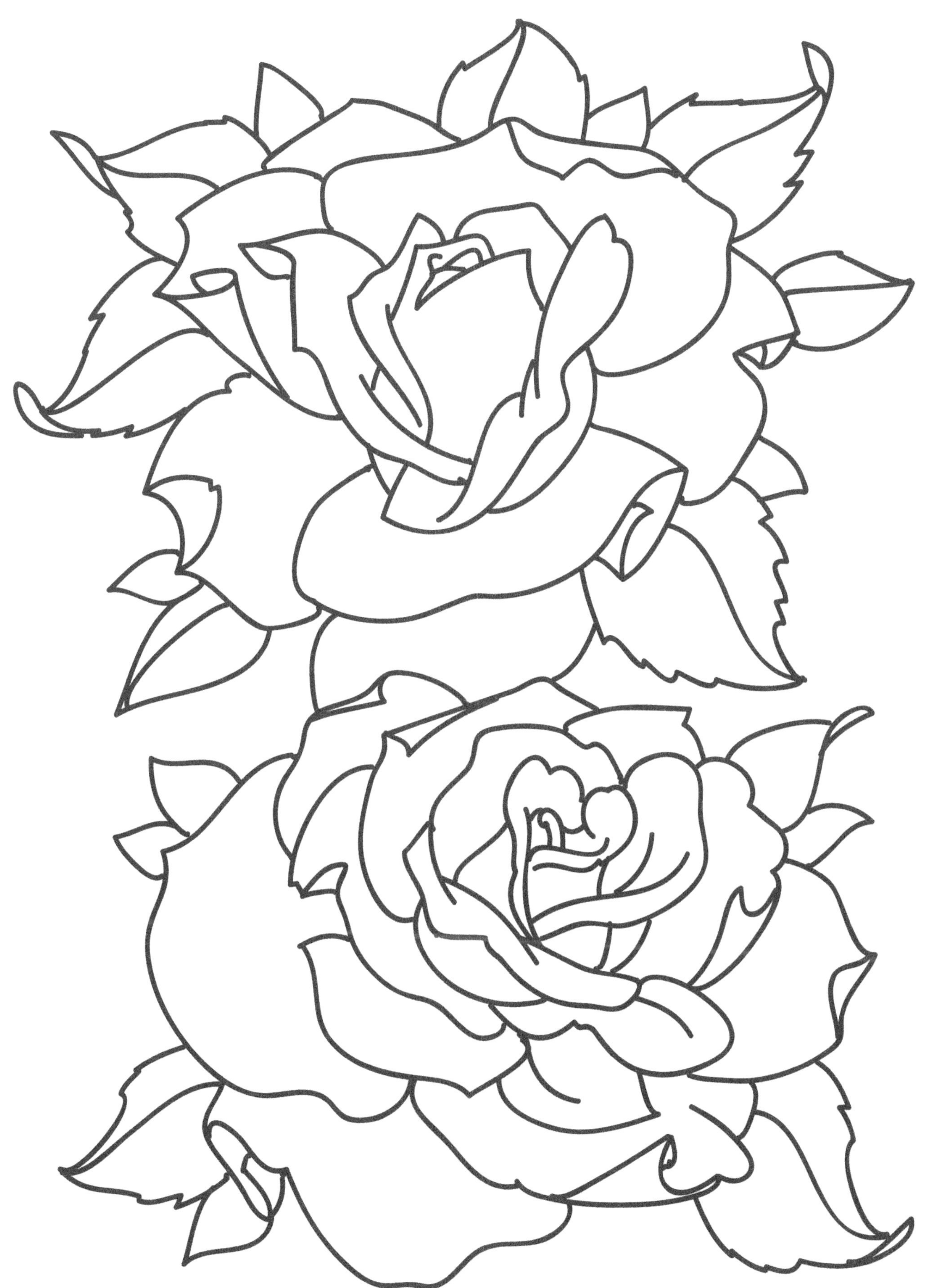

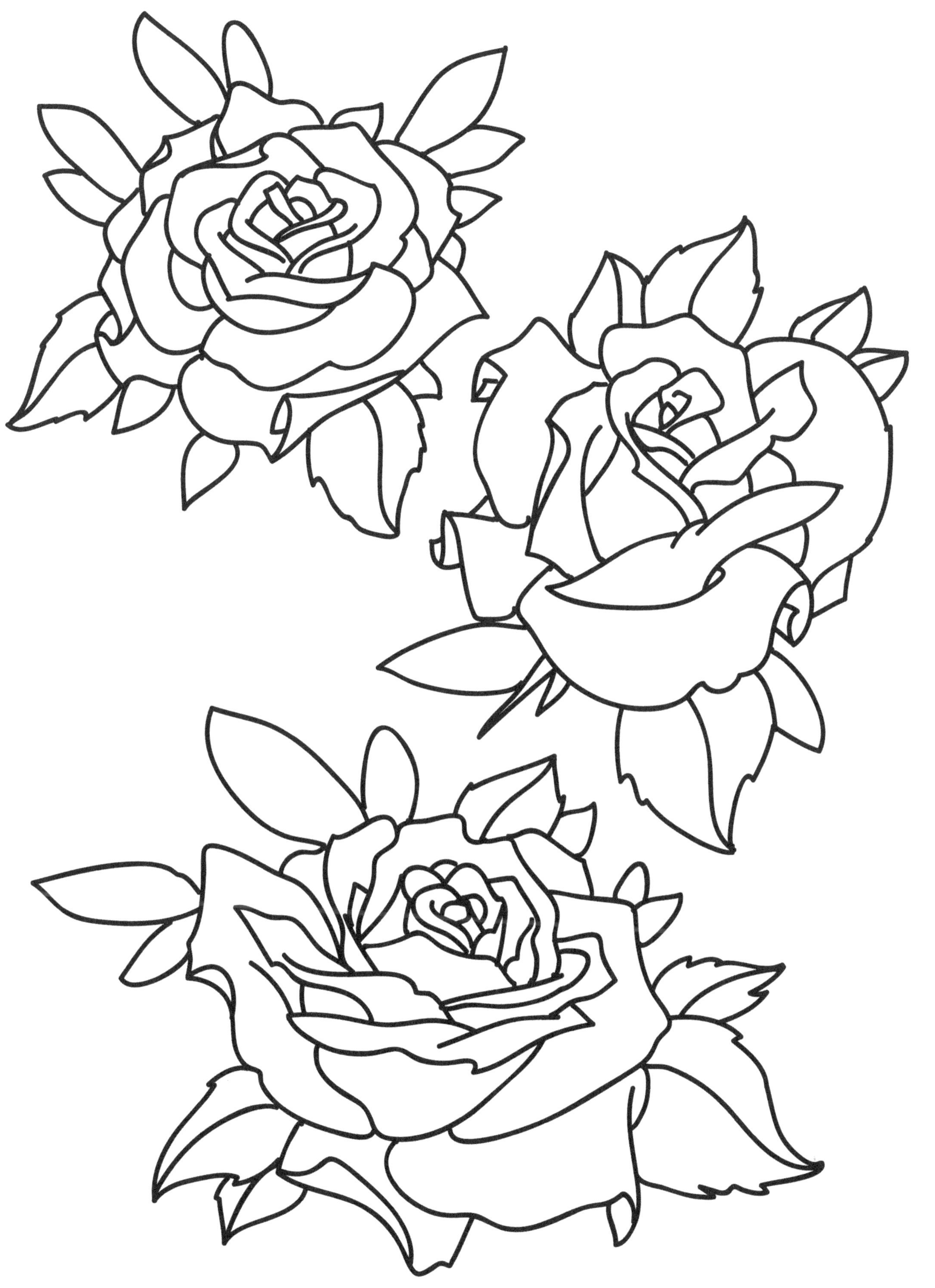

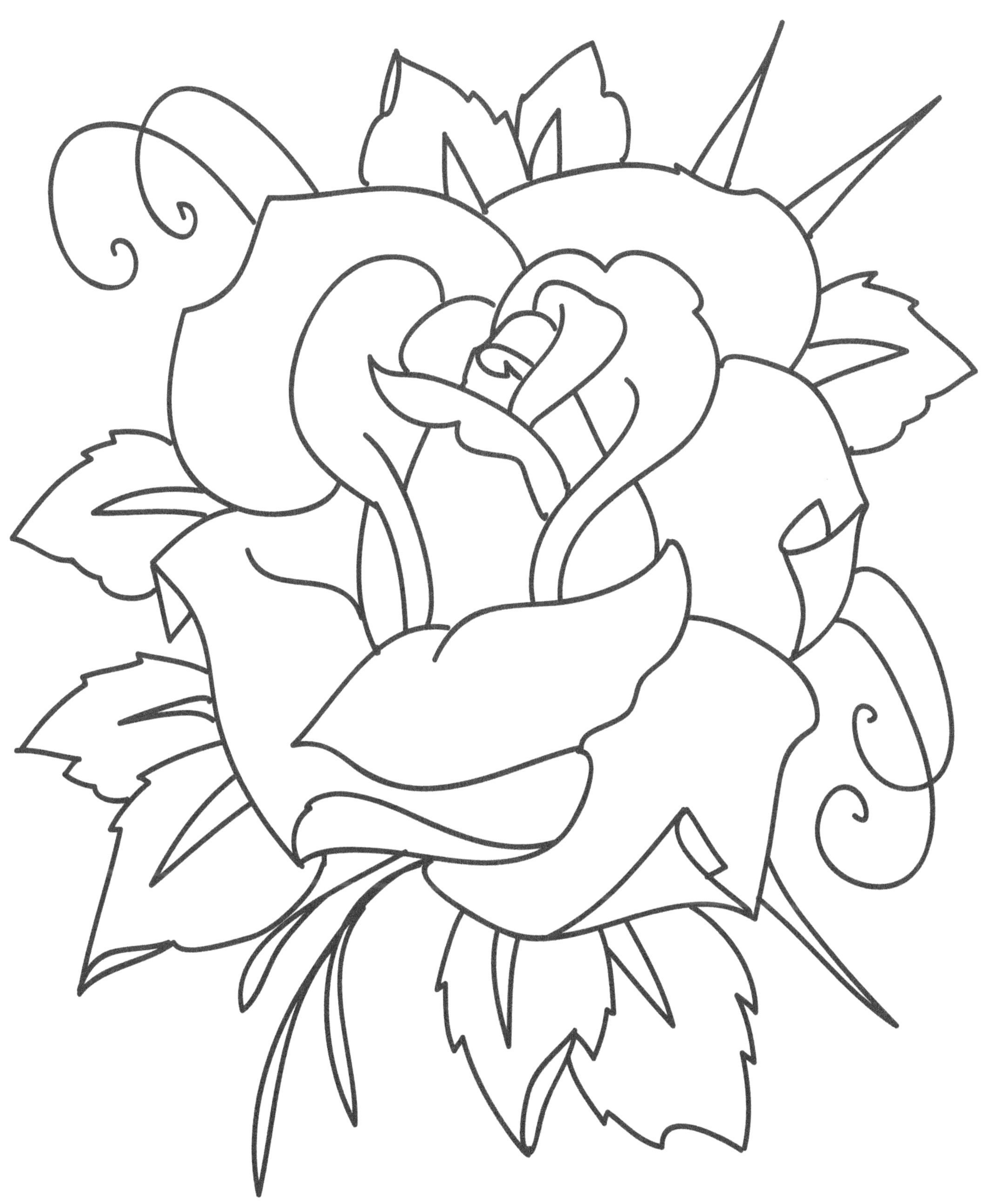

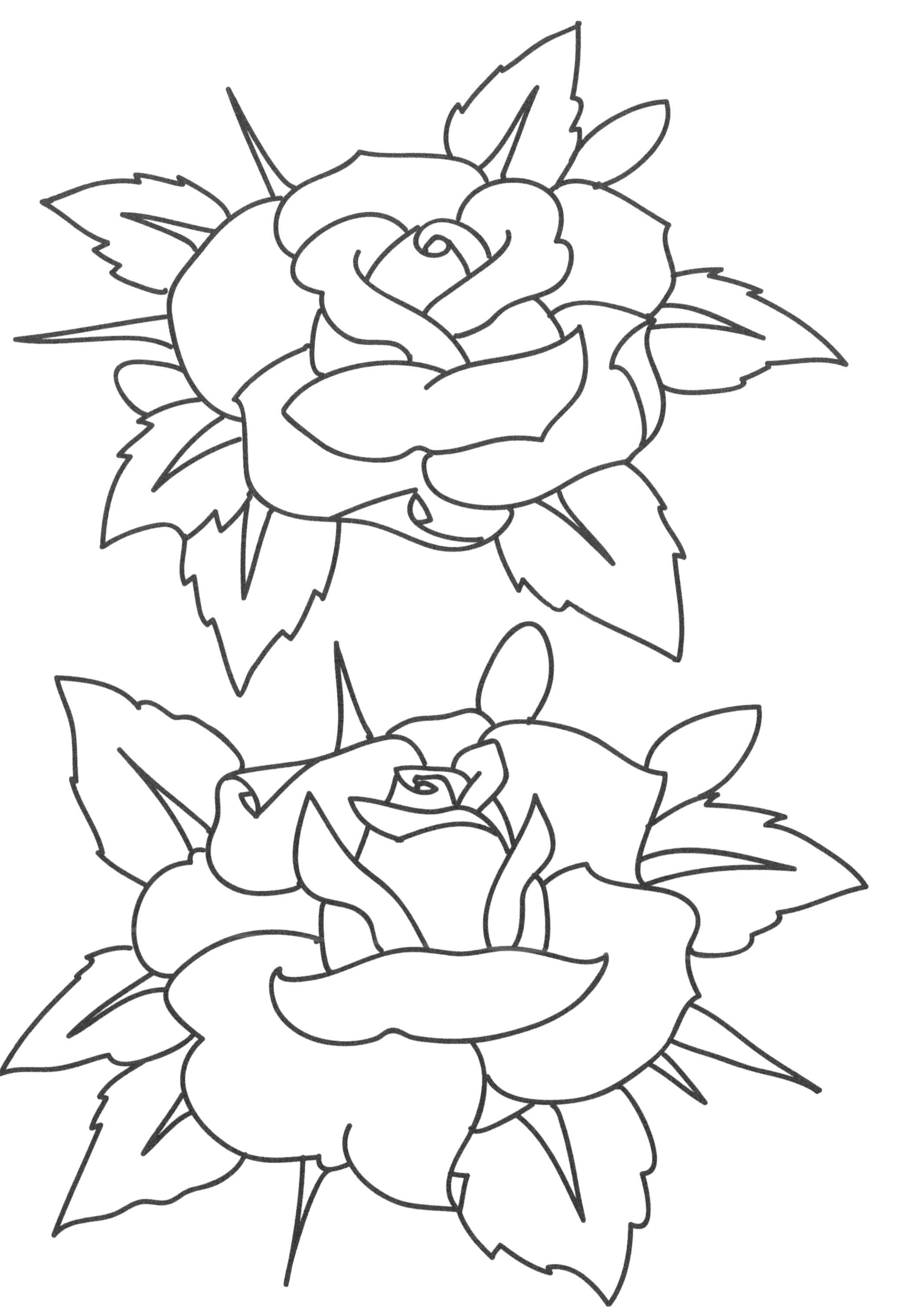

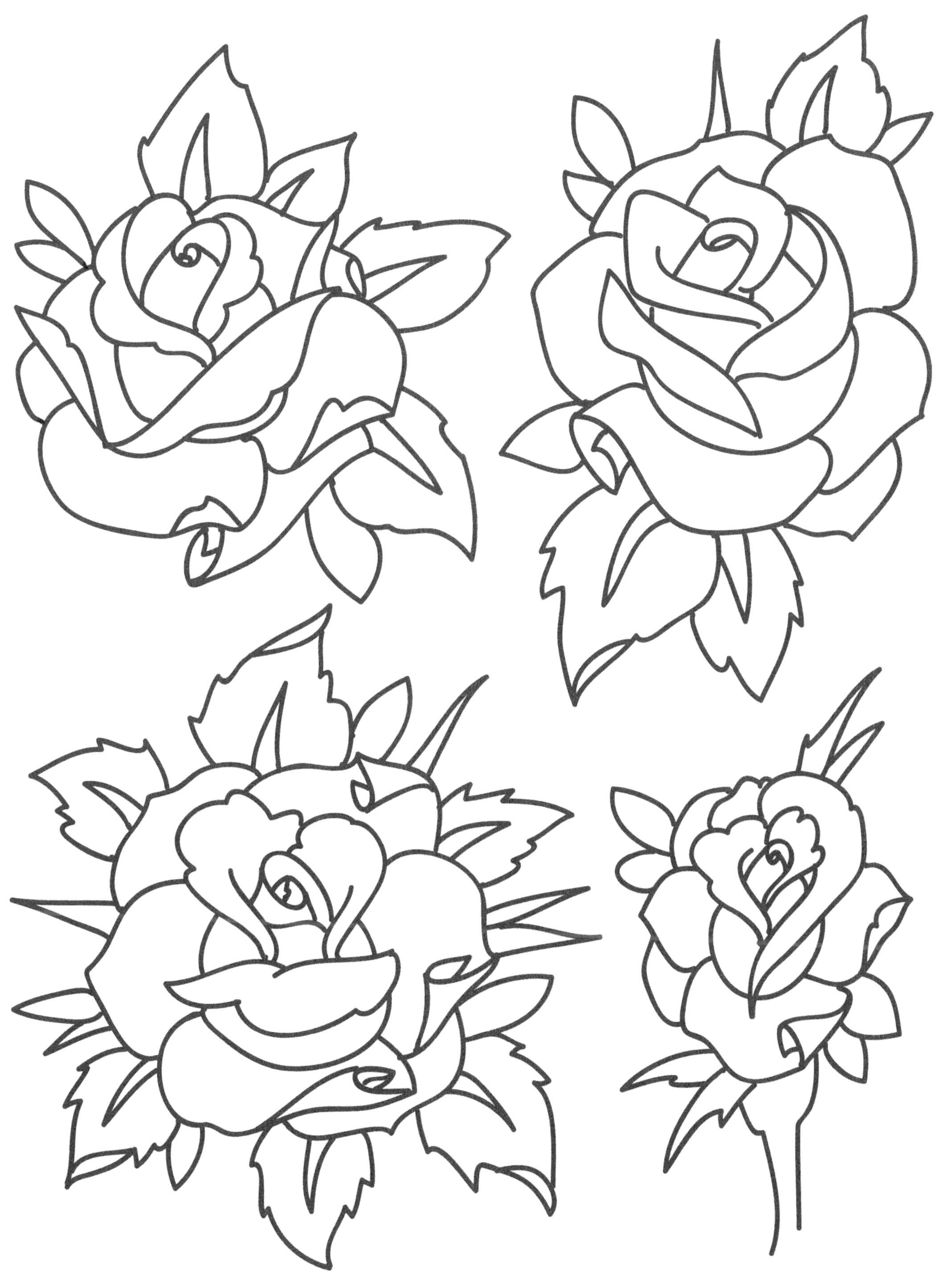

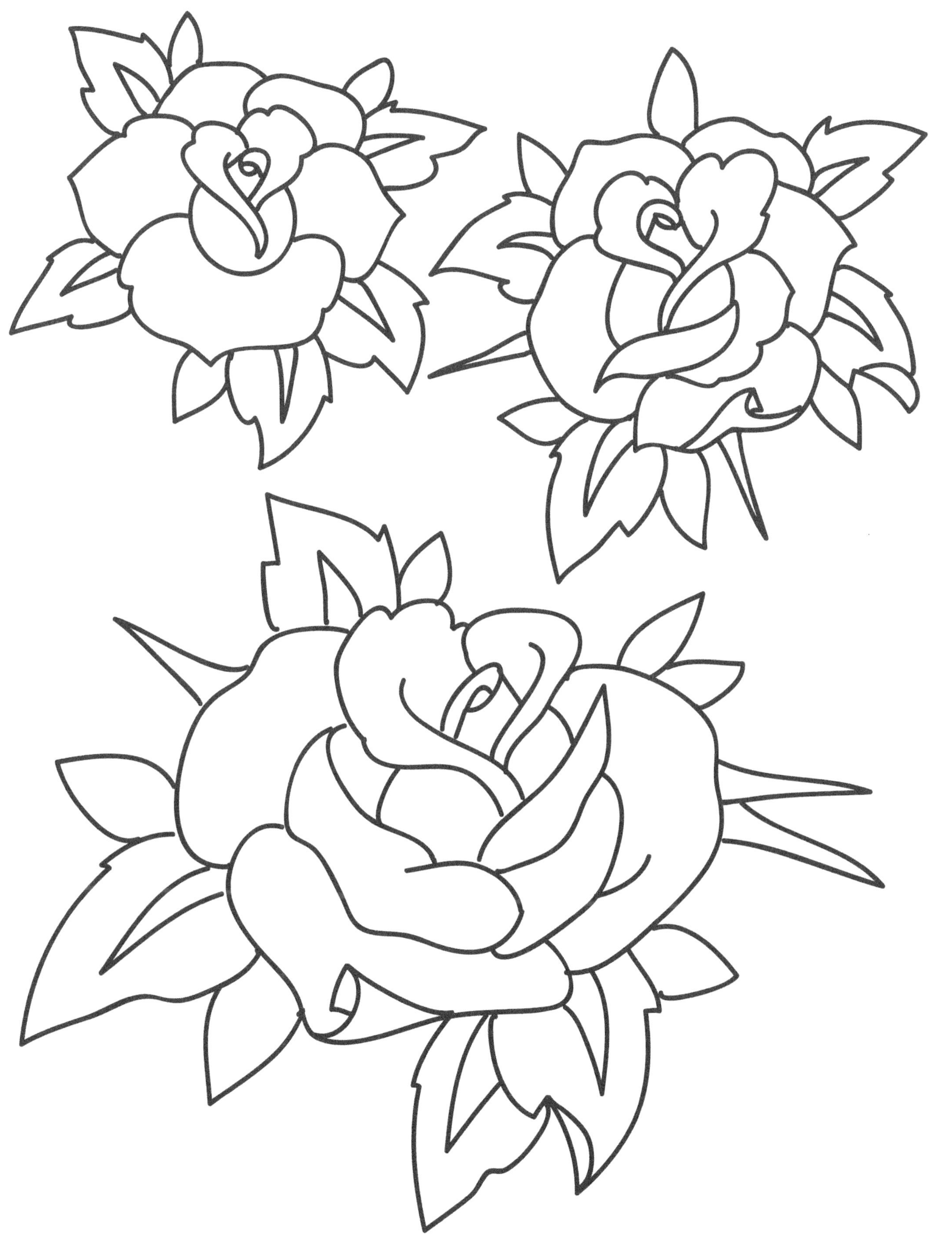

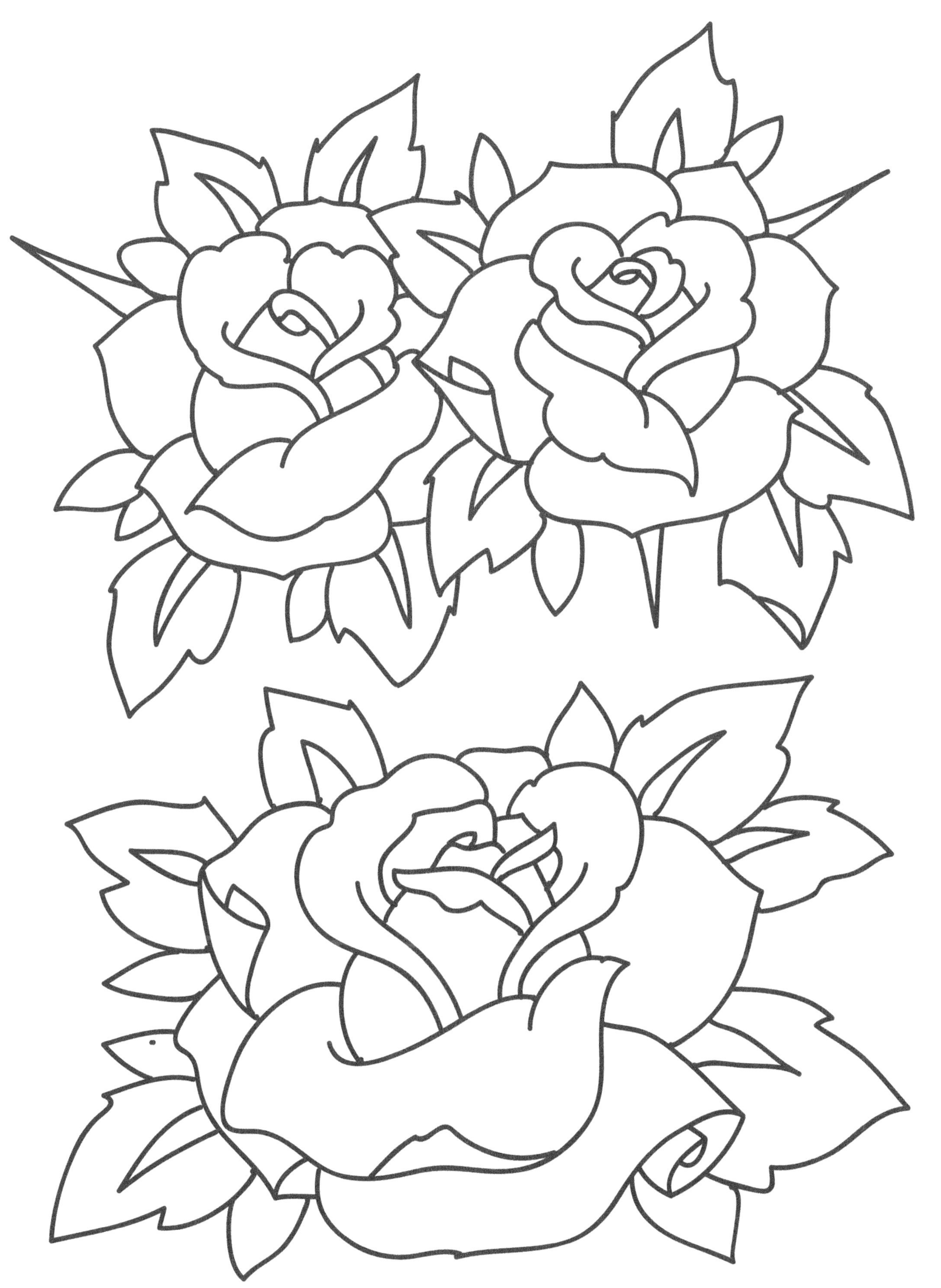

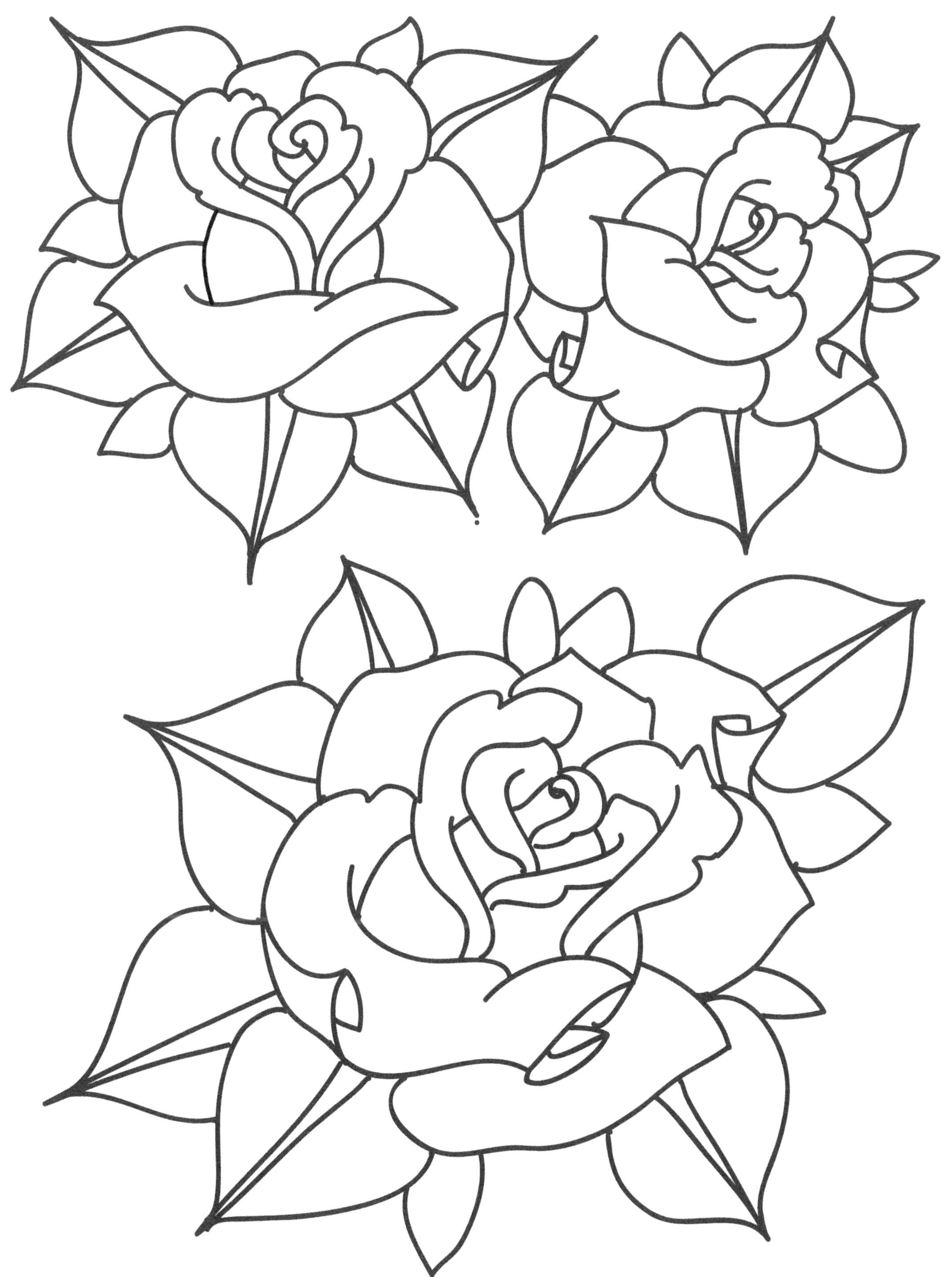

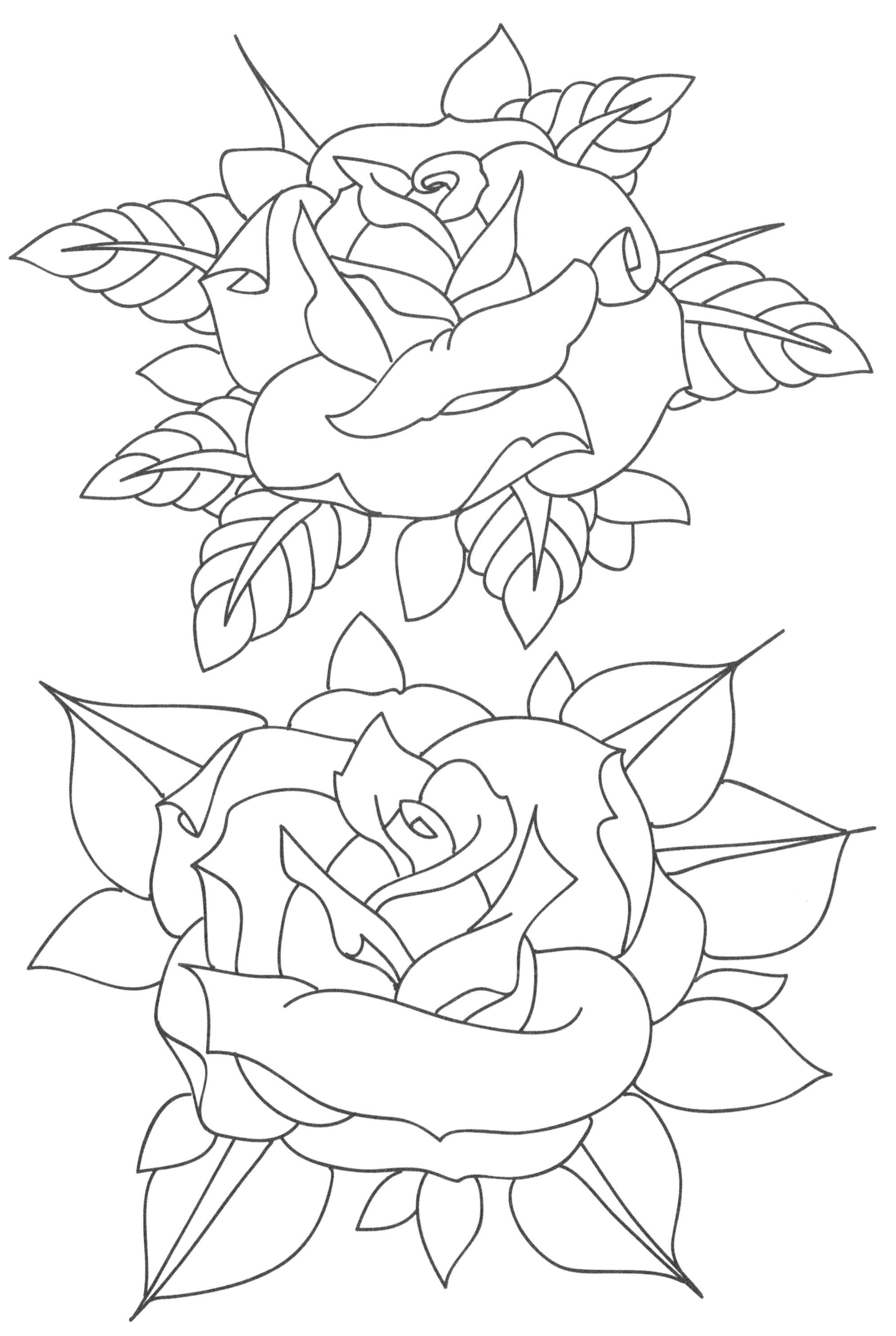

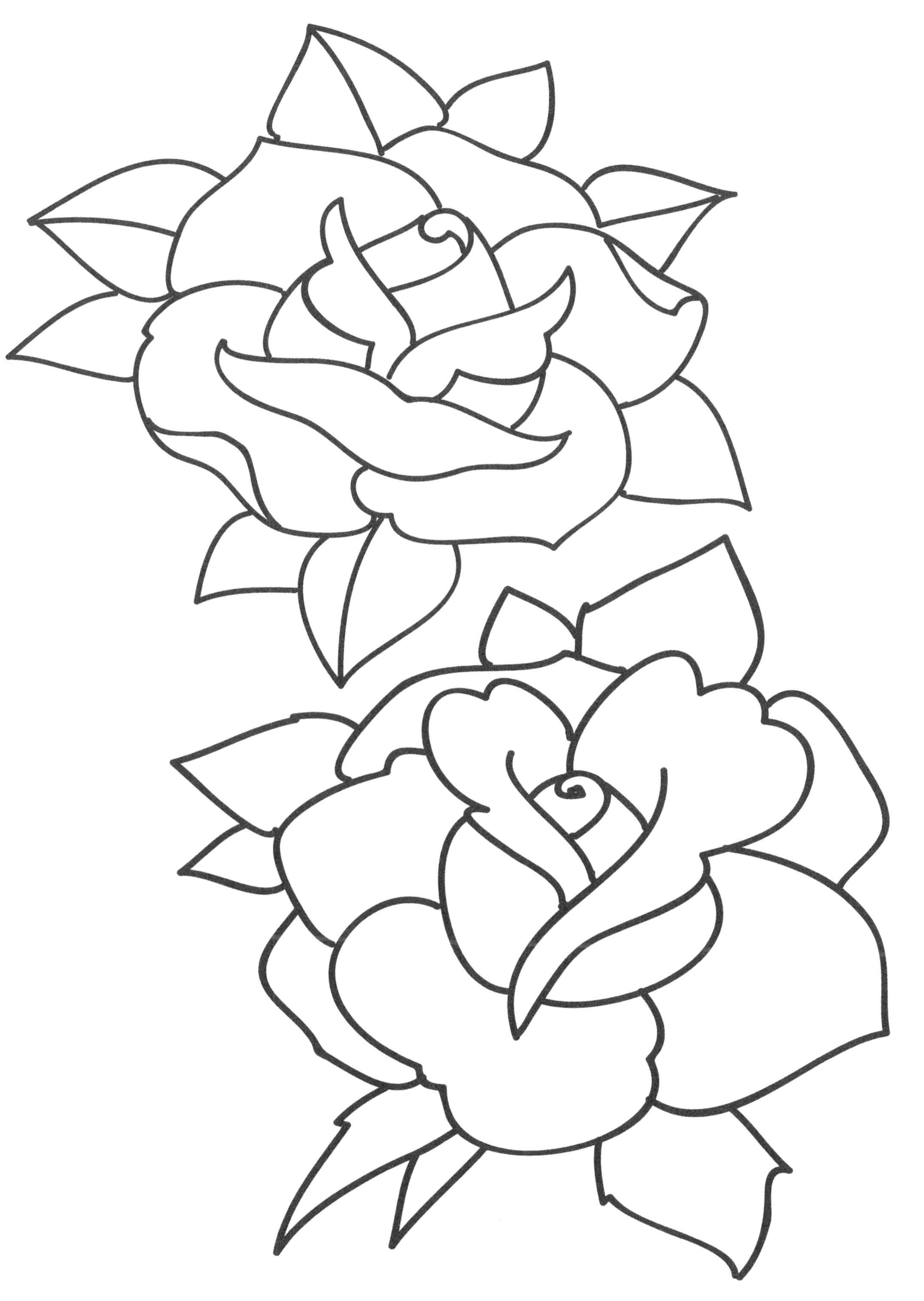

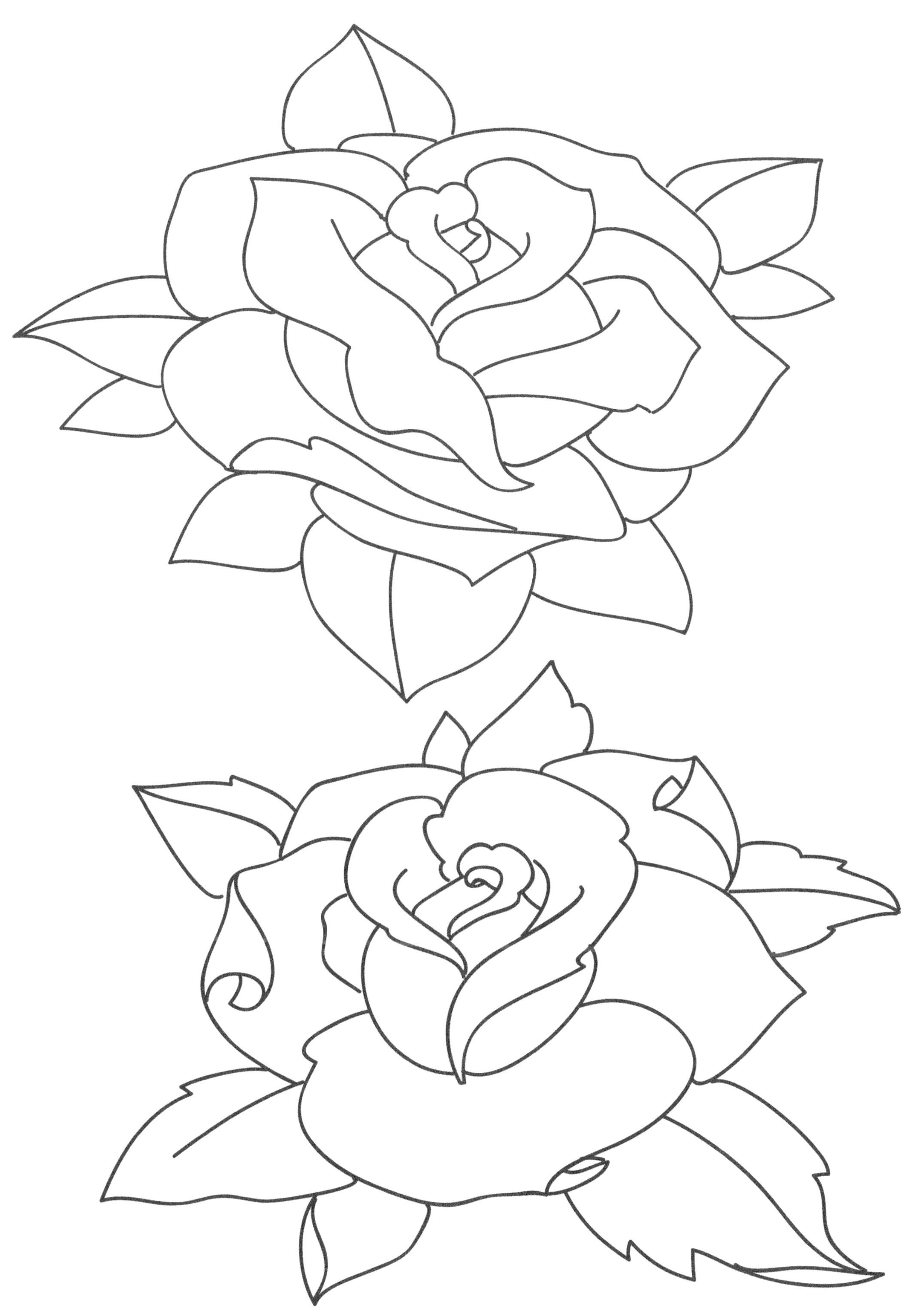

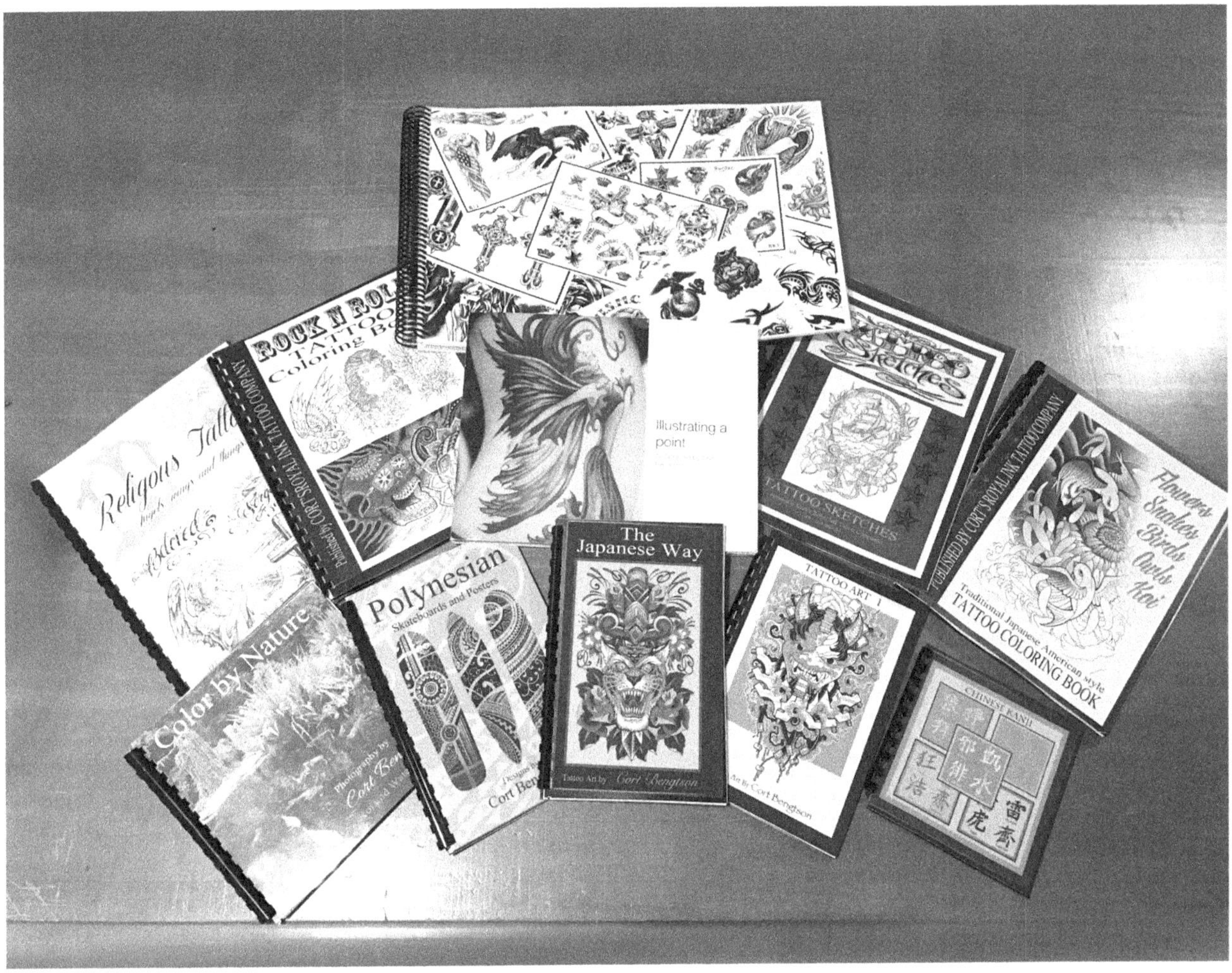

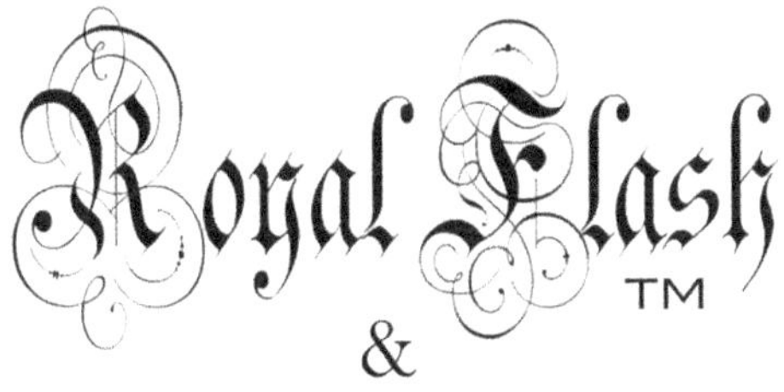

Check out these other great books,
Flash, Prints and original Art from

# Royal Flash ™

&

# Cort's Royal Ink Tattoo Company

@  royalink.631 on ebay

Contact us @  cortsroyalink@aol.com

See whats new @  cortsroyalink  on Instagram

# COLORKINGTATTOOS.COM

From Japanese style to surreal black and gray,
to watercolors and computer art, we have
something you will love. Prints
ranging in size from 11" x 17" to
40" x 50" will adjust the visual appeal
of any room.

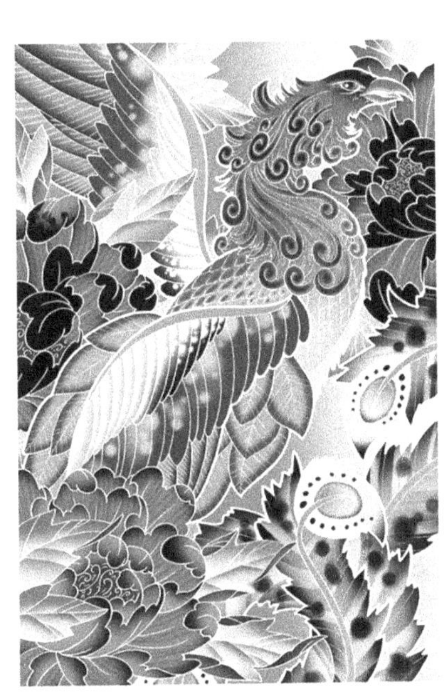
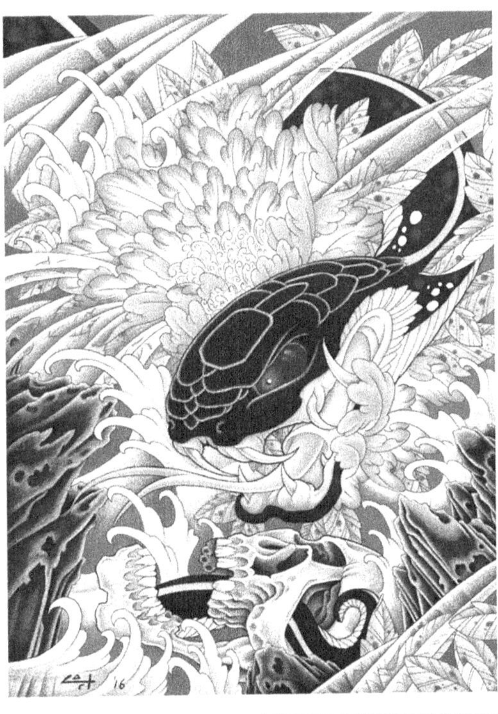
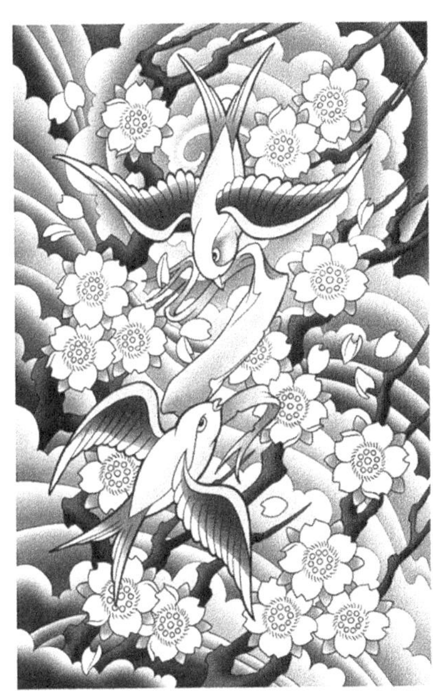
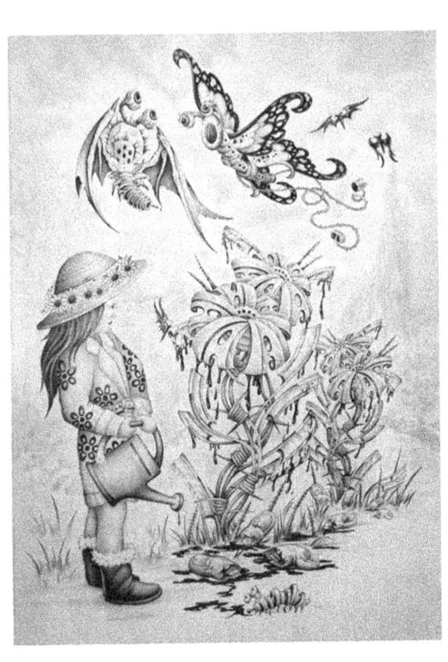
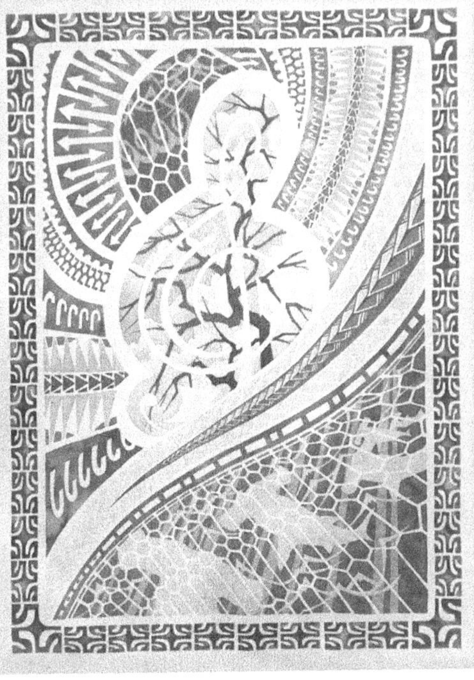
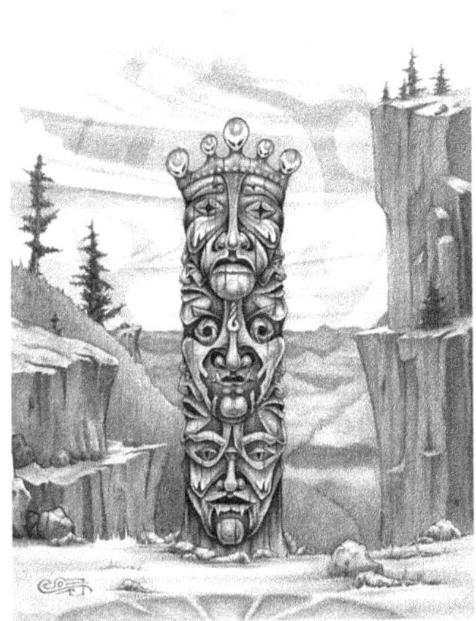